Strategies to Win

A Digital Marketing Playbook for Small Businesses

Christopher Mazurk

Mazloy LLC

ISBN 979-8-9920730-0-3 (ebook)
ISBN 979-8-9920730-1-0 (hardcover)
ISBN 979-8-9920730-2-7 (paperback)
ISBN 979-8-9920730-1-0 (audiobook)

For Mary who believed in me.

For my dad who blazed the trail.

For Steve who taught me about kindness.

Preface

Marketing sucks and strategy is a bummer.

But recognizing the right opportunity can yield unexpected rewards.

Let me tell you a story...

In the year 2000, an Atari Jaguar retailed for around $235, while a 1991 Geo Metro, depending on its condition, could be valued between scrap price and $900. I came across a Geo Metro in rough shape - bald tires, a trash bag for a back window, and, remarkably, a functional CD player as long as you pressed it just right.

At one time, that car would have been worth much more than the console. But the timing of things changes value. I happened to have both the car and console when their worth seemed roughly equal. So, I traded the Atari Jaguar for the Metro with a guy named Wade.

To be honest, parting with the Jaguar wasn't easy. The late '90s and early 2000s saw countless new game consoles, many of which barely left a mark, but a few - like the Sega Dreamcast and Atari Jaguar - were genuinely intriguing. Maybe that's why Wade accepted the trade, or maybe he just wanted to help me out. Years later, he would stand in my wedding party.

The Geo Metro carried me from Minnesota all the way back to California, the state where I'd spent my early years. As I drove west I thought about the Donner party when the trash bag flew from the back window and cold tore at my back like a junkyard dog chasing me out of Minnesota. I had come west, perhaps not as beleaguered as those who had come a hundred years before me, but my back and my left shoulder knew a dull, unforgiving chill from Nebraska to San Francisco.

I learned then that the lessons I was seeking would require effort - and I'd have to work for every bit of insight along the way.

Introduction

In 1996, I developed a website for a Lake Vermilion resort in northern Minnesota, working out of my father's Internet service provider. Building websites and computers for local businesses quickly became my passion. By 1998, I was working in my high school's computer lab, where a guest lecturer encouraged me to attend Bemidji State University. There, I helped design a minor in website development. But after a year, with the program still forming, I realized I needed a new challenge, which ultimately led me back to California.

I was driven by a blend of determination, willingness to learn, and a bit of youthful idealism.

Since then, I've watched the Internet evolve - AOL, Compuserve, Macromedia Flash, Adobe Flash, responsive design, ADA compliance, SEO, Google Adwords, ecommerce, and mobile-first design. The technology has shifted constantly, yet I've stayed engaged, working with countless clients, launching products, and leading several different web development businesses in one of the industry's most competitive spaces.

Networking became essential - meeting people, sharing ideas, finding inspiration. I stay curious about what's happening and who's making it happen.

Today, I believe in the journey that brought me here. I don't just trust in my younger self, who took a chance and headed west, or in the upstart who forged his way with more boldness than experience. I believe in the lessons I've learned along the way, the knowledge gained from my mistakes, and the value of data-driven decisions. These are the principles I've come to rely on for success.

This book embraces the fact that business rewards skill, dedication, and persistence. It's about creating success through intentional work and smart decisions, not empty bravado.

When you put in the effort, you win.

This book is about that journey - the path to establishing your company as a brand worthy of trust and respect. When you're communicating with anonymous people online, your brand needs to convey credibility and reliability on its own.

I wrote this book because, in my career, I've seen so many small business owners face the same challenge: never having enough time. Most started their businesses to support their families and give back to their communities, yet they find themselves constantly stuck on a hamster wheel, just trying to keep things running.

This book is packed with time-saving, proven digital marketing techniques designed to help small business owners build a marketing engine they can control - like turning a faucet on and off. My goal is to help them reclaim the hours spent on day-to-day tasks, so they can put that time back into what matters most: their families and their communities.

I want this book to make marketing *convenient* so you can have *fun*.

P.S. This book covers some technical subject matter. Consider referring to the glossary if you ever get lost.

Digital Marketing Primer

Maybe you're a small business owner who is trying digital marketing for the first time. Or, maybe you've been to the rodeo before. You don't want to gamble, or try and fail. And you want to know all you can about what to expect from the experience. Let's talk about what you should expect from your investment in digital marketing.

What Makes Digital Marketing Challenging?

Digital marketing is a blue ocean for most small businesses, an undefined or unknown market space.

Most small business owners have money for operations, but they struggle to invest in marketing. Traditionally, there are three reasons for this, and they all come down to cost:

1. Traditional marketing channels (print, TV, etc.) are too expensive.

2. Hiring and onboarding a marketing manager is cost-prohibitive.

3. There is not enough time to do the work yourself.

You'll notice that the last reason isn't directly related to dollars, but to *time*.

When everyone needs your time, you can't delegate work and you end up wearing every hat at once. And when you do start delegating the work, there's a lot of people with a lot of questions.

Further, most small business owners don't have the time to generate their own marketing plan, or even provide the relevant information to a marketing team.

And finally, most small business owners don't have the patience that marketing requires. It's really hard to be patient with marketing experiments when the money you're spending means you might need to wait to take your next vacation or hire your next employee.

For all of these reasons, I believe that small business owners who invest in marketing deserve a return that goes beyond money.

I want to give you your time back, too.

Why Does Most Digital Marketing Fail?

Effective marketing today goes beyond personal networks. It calls for structured lead generation, balanced sales and operations, and clear team responsibilities. To achieve sustainable growth, businesses need to be thought leaders while experimenting with new channels and messages.

We're witnessing an evolution of sales and marketing strategies for small businesses:

1. **Building the Airplane:** Small businesses are great at pivoting their focus. This creates short-term wins. It's also poisonous to marketing efforts.

2. **Traditional vs. the Internet:** Traditional marketing like personal networks and word-of-mouth can only go so far. The Internet opens new doors, but it needs formal lead-generation efforts to keep things moving.

3. **Sales and Operations Balance:** While operations managers know efficiency, they may lack the sales skills that drive growth. A balanced approach ensures both areas work together effectively.

4. **Playing to Positional Strengths:** Sales teams shine at closing leads, not generating them. Shifting their focus to closing can boost productivity and create room for formalized marketing efforts.

5. **Diverse Marketing Tactics:** From brand-building and digital presence to data-driven outreach, successful marketing requires aligning different approaches with both immediate and long-term goals.

6. **Scaling with Strategy:** Small businesses often need to move from a relationship-based, founder-driven approach to a scalable, structured one, which calls for adaptive leadership and investment in the right reporting tools.

Many marketing campaigns fall short because they lack a unified strategy and still lean on traditional techniques, overlooking the value of metrics and reports. Scattered marketing efforts and unbalanced team roles add to the challenge.

With focus, patience, and the right strategy, marketing success is within reach - and this book will show you how.

How Much Should Digital Marketing Cost?

The rule of thumb is that you should invest 10% of your annual revenue target into digital marketing.

Ideally, your profit margins are healthy enough to afford that. Some marketing experts also make compelling arguments for marketing costs to be based on profit, which also makes sense as a responsible choice.

Traditional marketing, word of mouth, and networking will take a long time to get you to a point where you can invest in that way.

At Mazloy, we spend 10% of our annual revenue on our marketing efforts. That's how we see growth, and that's what we recommend.

So with that said, most small businesses between $500,000 and $10 million in annual revenue should start out with an **organic marketing budget** of $2,000 to $3,000 a month.

That puts your annual budget at $24,000 to $36,000. Which, of course, is less than the 10% of annual revenue (or $50,000) recommended minimum.

So, where does the rest of the budget go?

Answer: **paid campaigns**. Google Ads, Facebook Ads, and other paid platforms give you the ability to drive traffic quickly to the experiments that you're running.

That said, the majority of your budget should go toward organic efforts. Those will pay off in the long-term, whereas the paid campaigns only last as long as you pay for them. They're a great way to give your organic efforts an early boost.

How Much Should You Spend on a Lead?

There are different ways to determine your Lead Value (LV) and countless calculators available. Everybody has their own way of doing it. What I'm going to outline is a derivative of Google's recommended method.

First of all, you have to start out with your Customer Lifetime Value (CLV). A lot of the aforementioned ways of doing this recommend using just an Average Sale as opposed to the lifetime value. That's a bit short-sighted. You're going to get a lot more out of a client than just that initial sale, so the value we use here should be representative of that. If you don't have the Customer Lifetime Value on hand, connect with your accountant who can pull the report from your accounting system.

The next thing that you're going to need is your Profit Margin (PM). The first step of the calculation is to multiply your Customer Lifetime Value by your Profit Margin percentage.

Then, you'll need to know your typical Close Rate (CR), the percentage of deals that you close. You can pull this from your CRM. For the calculation, take the result of the Customer Lifetime Value and Profit Margin multiplication, and multiply that by your Close Rate.

The final piece that you need, and this is one that most calculators tend to overlook, is your Referral Rate (RR). You should be getting some referrals from your clients. We want to make sure this is factored into the equation. To finish the calculation, you need to take the number you just created (your Customer Lifetime Value multiplied by your Profit Margin, and then all of that multiplied by your Close Rate) and add it to that same number multiplied by your Referral Rate.

This gives you the maximum amount that you should be spending per lead. We call this your Lead Value.

Here is the equation:

$$LV = ((CLV * PM) * CR) + ((CLV * PM) * CR) * RR)$$

As an example, let's say your Customer Lifetime Value is $10,000, your Profit Margin is 20%, your Close Rate is 10%, and your Referral Rate is 40%.

Your math would look like this:

$$LV = (($10000 * 20\%) * 10\%) + (($10000 * 20\%) * 10\%) * 40\%)$$
$$LV = ($2,000 * 10\%) + (($2,000 * 10\%) * 40\%)$$
$$LV = $200 + ($200 * 40\%)$$
$$LV = $200 + $80$$
$$LV = $280$$

You can use this to evaluate the success of your marketing campaign. It will help you determine whether or not you're getting the Return on Investment that you need to move the needle.

How Long Does it Take To Get Started?

It usually takes at least 90 days to get all of your marketing elements in place, which include:

- Clear messaging that speaks to your audience.
- A website with clear calls to action.
- Transitional and direct calls to action.

Your transitional call to action will be gated by forms that capture email addresses. Those transitional calls to action will expand your marketing efforts *if* they offer something of legitimate value to your customers.

This is always the hardest piece - putting out something that the customer will value.

Getting everything started, even if you're working with a marketing team, usually takes about 90 days. Even an experienced agency will have an onboarding process to maintain their profit margins and provide an efficient, effective service.

Of course, there are other books out there that recommend specific marketing strategies. Hopefully, because those techniques worked for the authors. But those will take time to set up, too.

And if you're doing it yourself, that 90 days isn't just three months of occasional side work. It's going to require a substantial time investment for you and your team.

For example, a good website will probably take upwards of 80 man-hours to complete, even without the transitional call to action.

You'll also need to get reporting and analytics in place and set up all the different accounts that entails.

And organic efforts take a while, which is why I recommend including paid ads in your budget.

There are a lot of steps to get your marketing foundation put in place.

How Long Will it Take to See Results?

Once you have the foundation in place, you can run multivariate tests. Those are the experiments that will make your marketing a scientific effort.

If you have all those tools in place, again, there are two ways that you can get started.

There's the paid route, where you can start to see results and traffic immediately. However, your cost per conversion is probably going to be higher than you want it to be.

Or, you can also start seeing high-quality traffic and conversions through organic Google placements and organic social media results. Those will probably take another three to six months to ramp up.

Marketing results can take time to appear, but you'll see how to earn some quick wins later in the book.

What Is Good Digital Marketing Today?

Today, good marketing isn't a gamble, a hack, or a door-hanger campaign.

Digital marketing is experiment-driven.

You start with a constant, which might be an existing website or landing page. You make one tweak, modify one variable, and drive traffic to your marketing tool so that you can measure the results, and then you adjust based on what you learned.

This is a process. It takes time. Unfortunately, most small business owners can't afford the patience to allow those changes to play out and accumulate.

But if you approach it with the right frame of mind, aware of your resources and how you can get the engine moving, opportunities are *everywhere*.

What is Bad Digital Marketing Today?

Maybe it would be better to call it "digital marketing in dreamland."

You see, many small business owners think that marketing today means going "viral" or finding the latest-and-greatest "hack" to make marketing work for them.

(Note: since you can't see my finger-quotes around "viral" and "hack," I used actual quote marks. But think of them as finger-quotes.)

An awful lot of small business owners who invest in digital marketing have this misconception.

There are lots of different "schemes" used in digital marketing.

The companies that are on top of those schemes early on find that other businesses will use them too. Eventually, everyone will start exploiting them, and if all your eggs are in that basket, then your business will stop growing.

Further, business owners who see marketing this way inevitably see the next "hack" as an all-in gamble - usually with the same disappointing outcome. These are high-risk marketing strategies and, since marketing is ultimately measured by the return on investment it's prudent to mitigate risk wherever possible.

Other small businesses are still marketing traditionally, through print, mailers, and other pre-Internet techniques. Or they're networking and meeting clients through word of mouth.

That's great! Because they're leaving that blue ocean just for you.

The smart bet is investing in a digital marketing foundation that will thrive regardless of the latest trends. And you can still do that today. The fundamentals haven't changed.

Yes, you have to look at marketing as a science and run experiments all the time. But that's always been true.

Now, networking and referrals can be effective - to a point. But relying on these methods means you're not growing your audience as effectively as possible, or even reaching everyone who might make a good customer. It's also a *lot* of time consuming work which lumps it into that high-risk category. Digital marketing expands your audience from the handful of people you can talk to each day to... well... everyone on the Internet!

Repurpose the time you spend networking to serve your clients, improve your operations, or go on that vacation.

That's why digital marketing is a huge blue ocean opportunity for most small businesses. And this book will help you reap those rewards.

Digital Marketing Abundance

I want to make sure we're on the same page when it comes to some key digital marketing ideas. At its core, digital marketing is about having an "abundance" mindset rather than a "scarcity" one.

If you believe there's only a limited amount of business out there, this book might not resonate. And if you often find yourself worrying about competitors taking your slice of the pie, this approach may feel a bit unfamiliar.

But consider this: what if there's more than enough business for everyone? What if opportunities are plentiful, just waiting to be tapped?

If that perspective feels right to you, we're off to a great start! There are just a few more foundational concepts to agree on so that this book can bring you the most value.

Be a Fisherman

So... you want to catch a fish.

If you know exactly what fish you want to catch, and exactly where that fish is, and that fish will provide all the sustenance that you need, you can go fishing with a spear.

You can aim for one specific, unique target and bring home the bacon. (Or fish. Whatever.)

What if you don't know exactly where that fish is? What if you don't even know what kind of fish there are?

You might be better off using a net to catch whatever's swimming in the area.

Digital marketing is a lot like fishing.

Spearfishing

Let's say your audience is connected to a very specific marketing channel. For example, you run a fishing boat company and everybody who wants to rent a fishing boat goes to one specific website to find out if your boats are available. If that's the case, then your marketing campaign can be pretty limited too. You can spend your budget on improving the conversion numbers on that website.

Unfortunately, that's not usually how digital marketing works. It's pretty rare for a company, especially one that wants to scale and expand an audience, to 'spear' enough targets via one marketing channel.

With all this in mind "net fishing" is usually the way to go.

Net Fishing

Now, a net takes more time to set up. You don't know exactly what you're going to catch. It's going to take more effort to reel it in and sort the good fish from the useless ones.

But you probably don't know which specific fish you want, let alone exactly where it is.

And if your fish aren't trying to jump into your boat themselves, you're a lot more likely to catch the right fish (which are leads, remember?) with a wide net.

Casting a wide net means marketing across as many channels as you possibly can.

If you find out that all your fish are coming from one net you can consider if spearfishing is a good option. Or, you can spearfish in that area and cast nets in other places. It's a big blue ocean after all. You just want fish.

So, what's the best way for a small business to market in as many different channels as possible?

In other words, what's the best way to see a return on investment from your marketing dollars?

That comes down to publishing a single marketing piece across as many channels as possible. For example, you can film a video that you publish to YouTube, use the audio for a podcast, pull 15 - 30 second clips for social media, and turn the transcript into a blog post. Use templates to structure the message and tools to automate the process wherever possible. This is called content repurposing which I'll cover later in this book. Work smarter, not harder. Right?

Be a Reliable Marketer

Effective digital marketing campaigns require two things. **Consistency** and **follow-through**.

Consistency

Your customers need to see you showing up at the same time over and over before they'll start to trust you.

On social media, for example, you need to post content regularly in addition to responding to the comments that your customers leave in a timely manner.

There's a boots-on-the-ground effort involved with social media to make sure that your audience continues to grow. You need to visit your customers' social media profiles, following them, liking their posts, and asking them to follow you. At a certain point you'll reach critical mass and that's where you're going to start seeing things really working. But that takes some time and consistency.

Consistency in your delivery will drive the engagement necessary for social media algorithms to put your content in front of your clients. You need to create the content, start to create the connections, and then things will start to really pick up. That could take three to six months of consistency for social media.

For another example, let's consider your Google search results. If you use tools like Google Search Console, you can submit the sitemap for your website, and it will get indexed very quickly.

But there's a difference between your site appearing on Google and Google *prioritizing* your website in search results.

For example, when somebody searches for your company's name, you'd expect to appear first, right? But that's not necessarily going to happen automatically. Even if your brand or company name is pretty weird. (Like Mazloy.)

The quickest way to expedite this process is to pay for ads that direct traffic to your website. Because Google pays attention to the number of visitors, specifically new and unique visitors, that make it to your website. But they also pay attention to things like how long those visitors actually stay on your website.

That's why you need to consistently publish content on your website that provides value to your visitors.

If you have enough content on your website you can drive traffic to it using paid ads. This will generate the volume of visitors you need to run multivariate tests properly. Then, you can adjust your website in a way that maximizes visitor engagement. This is when Google will start to really pay attention and rank your site favorably. If you're not consistently publishing content to your website and aligning your paid ad efforts with test cases you're leaving money on the table.

Follow-Through

But the thing that really takes time, and where the boots on the ground effort *reappears*, is developing links back to your website from other websites that Google knows are high quality.

Those links build your website's **domain authority**, which is the key metric for credibility and legitimacy in Google's algorithm.

Domain authority is measured as a 1-100 score. A website with a domain authority in the 50s or 60s, for example, looks much more legitimate to Google than a site with a score in the 20s, and those sites' position on a search results page will reflect that.

There are strategies for increasing your domain authority that I'll cover later in this book, but they take time and effort. Once you've done that, though, it makes all the difference in the world.

But that's just the strategy - you'll also need to create and publish content *consistently*. After that, someone needs to tell people that your website exists and has high-quality content, and invite them to come take a look and participate.

That's the follow-through. This is what most companies miss.

You see, if you start getting the right people to link back to your website, your domain authority will start to grow.

And as your domain authority grows, you're going to start to see the ranking of every page on your website increase in Google.

And when your domain authority is higher than your competitors', your listing will appear above theirs in an apples-to-apples Google search.

In short, you want your domain authority to be as high as you can get it. And that takes time and follow-through.

It's not like viral marketing, where you blow your marketing budget for the next 10 years on a great Super Bowl commercial (or a silly social media video). Viral marketing is like playing the lottery. It's bad marketing. It's marketing in dreamland.

Most people in the world don't win the lottery. If you're like most people your wins will come from being a reliable marketer. Make small, regular investments in your marketing, just like anything else in life. Keep feeding the "win machine" with delicious consistency and follow-through.

Tell Your Story

It's not that you or your company offers something for less money than somebody else. It's not that you do a better job than somebody else.

Your story is what makes you valuable.

Your story makes you unique.

Because no matter what people try to do, they cannot replicate your story.

Your story is a combination of two things:

1. Your truth

2. Your experience

Your Truth

Your company's truth, good or bad, agree or disagree, is the way that you view a situation. At Mazloy, for example, our truth is that marketing works in the way that I'm describing to you. And that is something that we firmly believe in. We believe that company-wide.

Another marketing company's truth might be that discovering and using the latest marketing scheme before the competition is the way to go. That's a black-and-white example, because even though we don't believe that, we have absolutely come across marketing companies that do believe that, and that is their truth.

So the first thing is your truth, right? Because it's not necessarily going to be completely unique, like a fingerprint, but it is going to be something that you're passionate about. The second piece is your experience. And this, when you add it to your truth, is what makes your story unique.

Your Experience

Your experience as a company can never be replicated by any other company, even though there might be many similar companies out there.

The clients you've had, the journeys you've gone on with those clients, the things you've learned with those clients, the industries and verticals those clients have been in, your successes and the lessons from your failures... those are all part of your journey.

That path is very specific to you and to what you shared with your clients. So even if you take another company that's very similar to yours, where your version of what is true and their version of what is true is the same, their experience and your experience will not be exactly the same.

When you add your truth to your experience and their truth to their experience, it creates a unique scenario that can be compelling and valuable to clients.

The Deli Analogy

Imagine two delis, each with a unique story.

Jimbo's Deli, for instance, has a strict rule: *no turkey in any of its sandwiches*. This isn't just a random choice; it's rooted in Jimbo's background, where turkey isn't appreciated. For Jimbo's Deli, their story is about being the place where turkey simply doesn't belong.

Right across the street, Turbo's Sandwich Shop has a different take - they won't add cheese to any sandwich. This is what sets them apart from Jimbo's.

Each deli has a story that reflects its own perspective and values.

Now, if you're looking for a sandwich, you might choose Jimbo's because you appreciate their dedication to quality meats without turkey. Or maybe Turbo's appeals to you because you love turkey but don't care for cheese. Alternatively, you could find a deli that offers both turkey and cheese if that's your preference.

The point is, a story can't be fabricated. A company's story is genuine and will resonate with customers who connect with its values. By owning and communicating your story with pride, you create a unique value that competitors can't imitate.

In digital marketing, your story is your standout quality. When you truly embrace it, you'll attract customers who are looking for exactly what you offer - authentically.

Share the Secret Sauce

Unless you're one of the rare companies, like Coca-Cola, whose entire brand hinges on a closely guarded recipe, sharing your process can be an asset. For Coca-Cola, their unique value is their distinct flavor, and the secrecy surrounding it enhances their appeal. But unless your value is tied to something you need to keep hidden, transparency is key to building trust.

Being open about how you do what you do lets people see your passion and expertise, which naturally positions you as a thought leader in your field. When customers sense your authenticity, they're more likely to trust you. And with trust, they'll feel confident that your goal isn't to "win" over them, but to create a win-win relationship. Transparency fosters the trust required for such a relationship.

In digital marketing, where anonymity is common, trust becomes even more essential. And the fastest way to build trust is through openness.

This book will walk you through executing powerful, efficient marketing strategies. These approaches aren't proprietary; you could implement them yourself or hire another company to do so. I'm sharing this knowledge because I believe in building trust with you - even if we've never met. Trust is a powerful, automatic connector.

The real "secret sauce" is being genuine and transparent. By giving that away, you gain something far more valuable - trust.

Own Your List

There are so many different digital marketing platforms that are free to use and publish content. You don't need to pay for Facebook, Instagram, LinkedIn, TikTok, or Twitter/X accounts. You don't need to pay for a YouTube account. You don't even need to pay to post blogs online. You can open up a WordPress account for free.

With that said, any followers that you gain on Facebook or Instagram, for example, or any engagement that occurs on those platforms is not yours. You don't own it. Your company does not own that engagement and does not own those followers.

That's why owning your list is fundamental for digital marketing.

Owning your list means having control to communicate however you want, whenever you want. It also means that nobody can take the list away from you.

Not owning your list means that you need to communicate within the rules set by the platform you're on (YouTube, Facebook, Instagram, etc.). It means that they can change the rules at any time. They can even close your account at any time - in which case you will have lost access to your entire list.

You need to convert your social media followers, or YouTube subscribers, or visitors from Google into actual leads. These are potential clients for your company.

To do this, we have to go back to that compelling transitional call to action.

That might be a great PDF, or an email series - something that people will trade for their contact information because it's got the secret sauce. It answers their specific questions.

If you own your list, you can do anything that you want with that contact information. Once people sign up and give you their email addresses, you can target them with more specific advertising. You can nurture them into paying customers.

Remember, if your customer communication is limited to social media interactions, you're relying on platforms that you don't own. Instagram, Facebook, and the rest are known to change their algorithms, and in some cases, they can even wipe out your followers. It happens more often than you'd think. That's what makes relying solely on any platform you don't own such a high-risk marketing strategy.

There are lots of stories out there - YouTube is notorious for this - about how a change to the way followers work wipes out 90% of a channel's audience, erasing millions of followers. If that was the foundation of your marketing, 90% of the value from your marketing efforts would disappear in an instant.

If you want to protect yourself from the whims of third-party platforms, you need to drive people back to your website and collect their email addresses. Eventually, you'll want more contact information like phone numbers, first and last names, and dates of birth, so you have the tools you need to enhance their customer journey. I'll touch on this later.

But the bottom line is you have to own your list. If you don't own your list, you're essentially renting your marketing efforts, not owning them.

The Elements of a Digital Marketing Strategy

Begin with the end in mind.

The "end" in this case refers to your goals. Typically, this is a revenue target. But it can be other things like subscriber numbers, how many new clients you want to sign up, and much more. What's important is that you start this process by defining that goal (defining the "end").

A sound digital marketing strategy requires clear, measurable goals.

Advanced analytics now allow us to track and visualize every effort, making it possible to quantify success. To truly benefit from this data, business owners must set binary metrics, like a specific revenue amount, that clearly indicate whether their efforts succeed or fail, with everyone involved aligned on the goals and their measurements. The essential metric? Revenue - not profit - because revenue closely reflects marketing's impact, while profit is influenced by additional factors like operations. This focus ensures a more straightforward, actionable measure of business growth.

Measuring Success

Measuring success requires aligning your content strategy with wildly important goals (WIGs), setting objectives using S.M.A.R.T. criteria, and tracking progress through a balanced mix of key performance indicators (KPIs), including actionable leading measures and reflective lagging measures.

Wildly Important Goals

At Mazloy, every strategy starts with a Wildly Important Goal (WIG). This *revenue* goal needs to meet the S.M.A.R.T. criteria in order to establish a scope for a marketing effort and for the data to be usable.

- **Specific:** a precise dollar amount.
- **Measurable:** you have the tools in place to calculate the results.
- **Assignable:** one person in your company must own the effort.
- **Realistic:** mindful of your actual, existing resources.
- **Time-related:** you've given it a deadline.

Key Performance Indicators

Establishing key performance indicators (KPIs) lets you track the effectiveness of your marketing efforts. KPIs can be broken down into two main types:

- **Lagging indicators:** Metrics such as sales or revenue, checked monthly or quarterly, to see the final impact on your bottom line.
- **Leading indicators:** Early indicators like website traffic or social media engagement, monitored weekly, which give you an opportunity to adjust if trends aren't meeting expectations.

Example: Imagine you're running a digital ad campaign aiming for 20 new sales per month. Your website analytics show that only 5% of ad clicks turn into contacts. By increasing ad impressions or improving the ad's appeal, you can impact this leading indicator and move toward your goal.

The Buyer's Journey

The best approach for small businesses is to use a multi-channel marketing strategy that targets customers across various stages of their journey.

The buyer's journey consists of four main stages: Awareness, Consideration, Decision, and Support.

Different channels work best at different stages, so choosing the right ones for each is crucial.

Awareness

At this stage, potential customers learn about your brand, often through channels like SEO, social media, and paid ads. Content marketing, such as blog posts or infographics, can also help attract new audiences. The goal here is visibility — making sure people know you exist.

Consideration

Once customers are aware of your business, you'll want to nurture their interest by sharing more detailed content like case studies, testimonials, or in-depth guides. Email marketing campaigns can keep your brand top of mind and encourage prospects to learn more.

Decision

At the decision stage, customers are ready to take action. This is where calls to action (CTAs) can drive conversions. Ensure your website, landing pages, and sales materials are optimized for quick, easy decision-making.

Support

After a customer makes a purchase, your work isn't done. A successful strategy includes post-purchase support, customer service, and ways to turn satisfied customers into repeat buyers and advocates.

The Marketing Funnel

Reports in the form of simple visuals are more effective than raw numbers. When I meet with clients to review their wins we visualize each marketing campaign as a funnel.

Marketing Channels

The top of the funnel represents your marketing channels such as Search Engine Optimization (SEO), Pay-per-Click (PPC), Social Media, billboards, radio advertisements, etc. - whatever it may be - whatever you're doing to spread awareness about your company - these channels feed the "top of the funnel."

Marketing Campaign			
Channel 1	Channel 2	Channel 3	Channel 4

Unqualified Leads

Potential customers will often learn about your product or service without your knowledge. They might see your commercial or visit your website from a public computer, but when someone expresses interest in your product or service, and you can track it, they enter the funnel and proceed to the next step. They become an Unqualified Lead. A lead because they're curious about what you're offering, but not yet qualified because they've given you insufficient information about themselves and their needs.

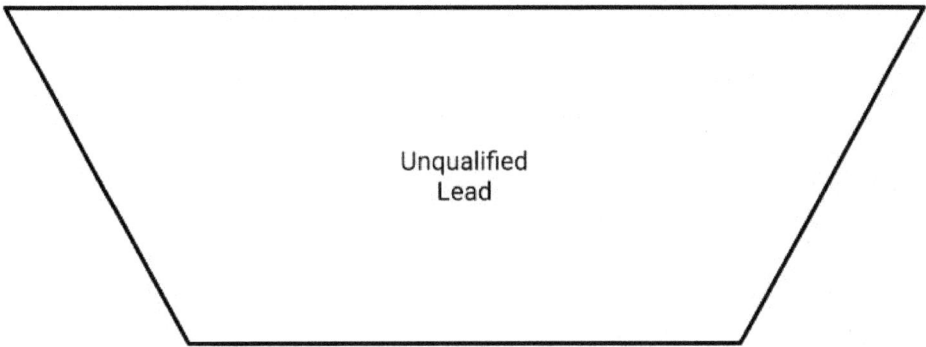

Unqualified
Lead

Marketing Qualified Leads and a Nurturing Campaign

When a customer calls your business or fills out an online form - something that enables you to get answers to specific questions - this will allow you to bucket the lead into one of three places.

First, if they're not a good fit for your company they can disappear from the funnel.

Second, if they seem like a good fit at this point they become a Marketing Qualified Lead (MQL). This means that your Marketing Team has confirmed that they might be worth your Sales Team's time.

Finally, your company may have a Nurturing Campaign in place which allows you to develop leads which are promising but may not yet be a MQL. Email Newsletters and scheduled follow-up calls are both examples of a Nurturing Campaign.

Here's where our fishing net comes into play. If you know you only want to catch fish over a certain weight you might make the holes in the net large enough for small fish to swim out. The larger fish ("Marketing Qualified Leads") will stay within the net where you'll then be able to determine if they're actually fish ("Sales Qualified Leads" - see below) or kelp.

The "Nurturing Campaign" comes into play when you consider that some of the fish may have squeezed through your net. They're pretty close to the size you want, but just a bit too small still. So, a smart fisherman will want to have a second net in place with holes a bit smaller than the main one. This way, you can go back and pluck the fish out once they grow to the proper size.

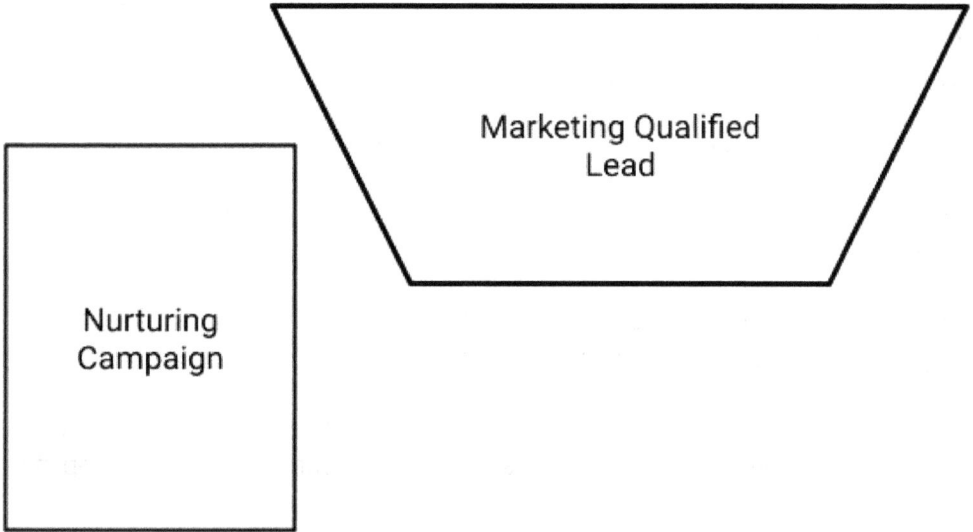

Marketing Qualified
Lead

Nurturing
Campaign

Sales Qualified Leads

If the lead passes through the MQL stage in the funnel you will have an opportunity to ask additional questions to determine if the lead is a good fit for your company. This may come in the shape of an additional form on your website or possibly a scheduled phone call with a member of your team. At this point, you'll probably ask more specific questions so you can better determine if you can help them. For example, if you're a personal insurance company you might need their Social Security Number so you can research their records.

Again, a lead can end up in one of three places at this point.

First, like with the MQL, if they're not a great fit they may disappear from your funnel entirely.

Likewise, there may be an opportunity to develop them into a better fit so you may send them to a Nurturing Campaign.

The final option, a result of the lead passing all of your tests, is that they become a Sales Qualified Lead (SQL). This means it's time for your sales team to step in and close the deal.

Best Practice Tip: It's easy to be tempted to combine the MQL and SQL stages into a single form or phone call. However, it's usually necessary to develop the lead a bit before asking the questions necessary to determine if they are a Sales Qualified Lead.

It's like dating - if you approach someone at a bar you can ask for their name and phone number but they'll probably be put off if you ask for their Credit Score. Meanwhile, you may be much more comfortable asking for that information after you get to know and trust each other more. That is - if their Credit Score is an important factor in determining if you want to continue dating them (hey...whatever floats your boat). This is why most online forms only ask for:

- First Name
- Last Name
- Email Address
- Phone Number

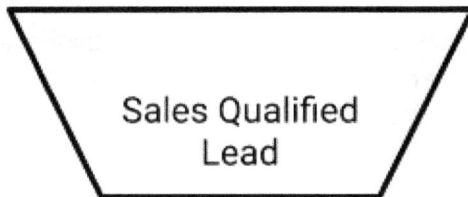

Sales Qualified
Lead

Close

This stage of the funnel is tricky, which is fitting seeing as it's the one step separating the WIG (revenue) from your marketing efforts.

In the other stages we are able to configure automated tools to track results. For example, we can track the transition from an "Unqualified Lead" to a "Marketing Qualified Lead" via a form on a website or a trackable phone number. These tools give us specific information about the number of visitors who enter a page vs. the number who complete the form or place the call. We know how each prospect found their unique phone number, we know the entry point and method of each website visitor. In other words, we can track conversions down to the individual transaction, giving us tremendous insight into how the process gestates and what components are sound. We can also handle attribution (e.g., giving proper credit to the effort responsible for a lead) programmatically. Remember, this is an age where we can track almost everything, attribution is an example of how that data can become insights.

The "Close", as a marquee player in this drama, is a unique animal that portends to buck trends that color the rest of the process. Sure, you track your SQL to close ratio, you develop "a close" which is part of your "sale", but to be honest, the close is entirely reliant upon the infrastructure and protocols in place at a given company.

The close is where the visitor enters your sales pipeline. Unless you (and your entire team) are diligent about defining and tracking the sales pipeline's granular movements, you'll find that this is the stage where the data has an opportunity to break down a bit or at the very least succumb to various forms of ambiguity. One example of this is customer contact logs. Sales Rep A might use narrative to track his customer correspondence whereas Sales Rep B may use a series of his own gates (similar to our funnel). Neither of these methods is more correct than the other, the issue is their lack of consistency across the enterprise. This is what makes the data difficult to define and leverage.

Fortunately, it's still very possible to interpret basic information in a meaningful way. We'll still know how many leads enter this stage and how many come out. We may simply find that attribution tracking gets a little tricky as human error becomes part of the equation.

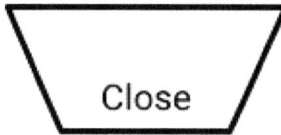

Close

Revenue

We've made it! This is the final, and most exciting stage in the funnel. Your Wildly Important Goal! You've done the work and can now reap your rewards.

This stage is straightforward… we track any activity that generates revenue.

Ideally, you'll want the sale to be represented by a single number which, in turn, represents your revenue. To do this, you need to know what your average sale is.

It is not absolutely necessary, but it makes the "at-a-glance" math easier. It allows you to assign a dollar amount to a lead all the way through the funnel instead of converting it in the last step. This may sound counterintuitive, but it creates more meaningful sales projections in the aggregate. Because you know your conversion rates through each stage of the funnel, and because you are using the average sale value as a constant, you can project revenue for a desired period, at will, with some accuracy. The degree of accuracy is totally dependent on the accuracy of your average sale calculations and the absence of wild, unpredictable fluctuations in conversion rates through the funnel stages.

Good average sale calculations only require good bookkeeping, math, and sampling, but funnel stage conversion can be deeply affected by attrition, hiring, force majeure, one-time market events, and other variables. It is best to mitigate factors that will make developing predictable conversion rates challenging, unless of course said factors will improve rates permanently or for a predictable term.

WIG

Visualizing the Funnel

All of these stages can be combined into a single funnel. The "Marketing Channels" sit at the top of the funnel. The purpose of this stage is to spread awareness about your company. At this stage, leads will be "cold" (meaning, they're not yet likely to result in a sale or you are unaware of them all together).

A percentage of your cold leads will advance to the "Unqualified Lead" stage, usually by clicking on a link and landing on your website. They've expressed interest by taking this action but you don't yet know who they are. They're starting to warm up a bit though.

If they call you or send in a contact form they become a "Marketing Qualified Lead". You still don't know much about them (again, you're on one of your "first dates" here) but they are orders of magnitude more likely to turn into a sale than they were at the top of the funnel. They're warming up. Also, since you have their information you can enter them into your "Nurturing Campaign".

To get to a "Sales Qualified Lead", you'll want your prospect to answer questions you might not ask on the "first date".

For example, the goal of a paid media marketer is to keep a client as long as possible. They spend a lot of time and money getting clients to sign up in the first place, and onboarding new clients into their systems. So, their profit comes from retaining clients. Because of this, smart paid media marketers have tools to analyze the potential for a successful campaign. These tools require answers to questions like, "what is your customer lifetime value?" and, "what is your profit per customer?". These aren't questions you can ask someone before you get to know them a bit. On the flip side, these are definitely questions you should ask before spending valuable resources on pursuing a lead. You want to make sure the lead is starting to get hot.

It's a good idea to think through these questions and capture the information via a second form on your website (that you only send to "Marketing Qualified Leads") or a checklist you cover during a phone call. The correct approach depends on the way you want to interact with your clients. Forms are the easiest to automate the process and capture the data, but they lack a personal touch.

If the "Sales Qualified Lead" passes the tougher questions it probably makes sense to connect them with a member of your sales staff. They're red hot to the touch at this point. This moves the lead into the "Close" stage. Again, it's to your benefit to implement systems and procedures which will minimize the opportunity for human error. A CRM with required fields is an example of this. You can mandate that sales people take specific steps during the "Close" stage and enter specific information at each step.

Best Practice Tip: Consider creating a second funnel for the "Close" stage which you analyze during sales meetings. Whatever process you arrive at, it's important that all of your salespeople define and record information in the same way.

Finally, if everything works out you're in the "Revenue" stage. Congratulations!

The funnel is a powerful tool as it breaks the marketing process into specific stages which allow meaningful analysis. If you generate 100 "Unqualified Leads" per day through your "Marketing Campaign" and only 1 of those leads fills out the form on your website to become a "Marketing Qualified Lead", you might consider spending some time improving your website. Perhaps the User Experience (UX) is confusing, or your form asks questions that make the visitor uncomfortable. There are tools like HotJar to help you pinpoint the issue. The funnel makes way to powerful strategic conversations which move the needle.

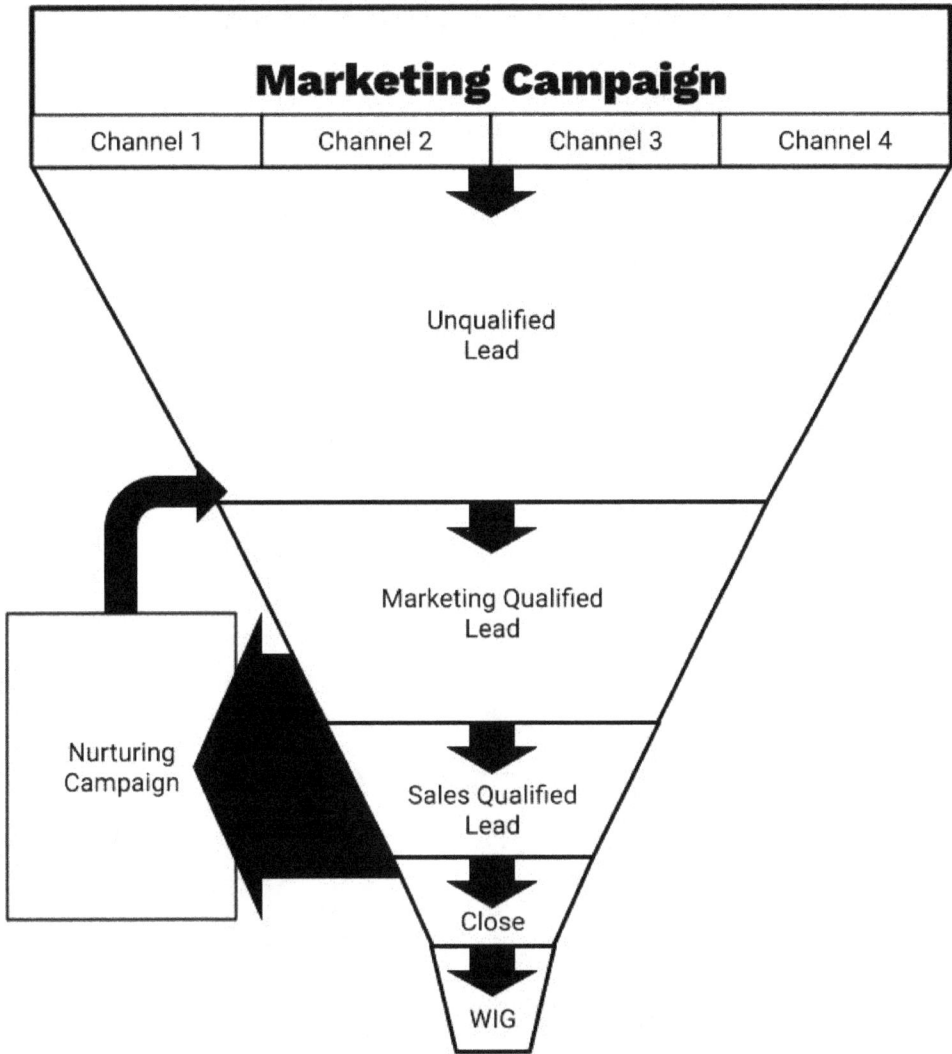

Digital Marketing Setup

In today's digital landscape, building a solid foundation for your marketing efforts requires a deep understanding of who your customers are, what resonates with them, and how to ensure they can easily find you. This section covers the components you need in place to attract, engage, and convert your customers effectively.

Buyer Persona

A good marketing strategy begins with clarity around your audience, goals, and message. It's not just a one-size-fits-all approach but a detailed plan that focuses on reaching your ideal customers effectively. The most effective strategies take the time to define a buyer persona — a comprehensive profile that represents your ideal customer. This persona drives all future marketing decisions and ensures every message resonates with the people who are most likely to buy your products or services.

Developing a buyer persona involves several key steps:

- **Identify demographic details:** Define characteristics like age, income, and location, specific to the audience you want to attract. For instance, if you're a business-to-business (B2B) company, you may focus on company size, job titles, or annual revenue. A business-to-consumer (B2C) company might look at factors such as household income, lifestyle, and spending habits.
- **Analyze behavioral traits:** What motivates your customers? What challenges do they face, and how does your product solve these? Understanding these factors can shape your messaging.

Example: Suppose you're a fitness brand targeting professionals in their 30s with busy schedules. Your marketing could focus on the convenience and effectiveness of quick workouts. The imagery should reflect relatable scenarios, such as someone working out at home before heading to work. In contrast, using pictures of a college student at a gym might not connect with this audience.

Using free resources like HubSpot's buyer persona tool can simplify the creation process, providing a clear foundation for every marketing decision.

Messaging

A useful marketing message is told from the perspective of the customer's story. It includes six essential steps:

- **Identify the customer's problem:** Begin by outlining the pain points, the challenges they want to overcome, your product or service addresses.
- **Introduce your company as the solution:** Show your customers why you're the right solution, emphasizing how you help them achieve their goals.
- **Offer a plan to succeed:** Detail the steps or benefits customers will experience when they choose your business.
- **Specify a call to action:** Prompt potential customers to take specific actions, such as contacting you or signing up for a trial.
- **Highlight the benefits of success:** Illustrate how life improves with your service, fostering confidence in the purchase decision.
- **Show what's at risk if they don't act:** Highlight missed opportunities to emphasize the value of choosing your business over competitors.

Tip: Avoid talking solely about your company's achievements. Instead, keep the focus on the customer's experience and how their lives improve when they engage with your product or service.

The C.A.P.S.S. Technique

The C.A.P.S.S. Technique can be the most powerful marketing tool in a business's toolkit. It provides a structure for the story you tell with things like case studies and testimonials. The story of how your business solves specific problems, helping potential clients understand the value you bring to the table.

In this section, I'll cover what The C.A.P.S.S. Technique is and how to use it for case studies and testimonials. I'll also explain why case studies and testimonials are essential, and how to create ones that resonate with your target audience. By following a structured approach and focusing on real results, you'll craft case studies and testimonials that build trust and attract new clients.

The Structure of The C.A.P.S.S. Technique

A strong case study or testimonial follows a specific structure to convey information clearly. The C.A.P.S.S. technique is an effective framework to ensure you include all essential elements:

- **Call to Action:** Make sure you end with a clear invitation for the reader to take a specific and urgent next step, whether contacting you, scheduling a consultation, or exploring more about your services.
- **Audience:** Define your audience. Be as specific as possible about who would benefit from the case study or testimonial, considering demographics like industry, role, or company size.
- **Problem:** Describe the problem your client faced in detail. Explain how it impacted their business and why a solution was needed.
- **Solution:** Show how you addressed the problem. Detail the steps taken and the strategies used without directly selling your business during this step.
- **Success:** Showcase the results, using measurable outcomes if possible. Paint a vivid picture of what your solution achieved for the client.

What is a Case Study?

A case study is a detailed examination of how your product or service helped solve a real problem for a client. By highlighting the issues faced, solutions implemented, and results achieved, case studies become a narrative that demonstrates your capability and expertise.

For instance, think of a case study as a success story. A lawyer may present a case study on a client's winning legal battle, while a marketing firm might showcase how it helped a client improve their brand's online presence. Ultimately, a case study is about showing potential clients what you can do for them, building trust through examples of past success. Case studies are valuable because they take complex information and make it accessible, allowing readers to envision similar successes for themselves.

What is a Testimonial

A testimonial is a statement or review from a satisfied customer highlighting their positive experience with a product, service, or company. Testimonials build credibility and trust by showcasing real feedback from past clients. They often emphasize the benefits customers experienced, how the company addressed their needs, and the quality of service received. Effective testimonials typically include the client's name, photo, and sometimes their business or position to add authenticity. Well-placed on a website, they help convert potential customers by showing proof of value and reliability.

Why Are Case Studies and Testimonials Important?

Case studies and testimonials play a crucial role in marketing because they help build credibility. By providing real-life examples, you show potential clients that you understand their pain points and can deliver results. This trust factor is critical, as customers are more likely to engage with businesses they believe are trustworthy.

Moreover, case studies and testimonials simplify the decision-making process. Prospective clients often want proof of effectiveness before committing to a product or service. For example, a well-written case study demonstrates your ability to solve problems, making it easier for clients to see the benefits of choosing your business. Case studies and testimonials are especially powerful for B2B companies, where decision-makers rely on detailed information to make informed choices.

How to Write a Case Study with The C.A.P.S.S. Technique

Testimonials are far more straightforward than case studies as your clients ultimately provide the content. Structure the questions you ask them according to the "Problem", "Solution", and "Success" criteria above. Then, let their words do the rest.

Writing a case study involves more than just presenting information. It's about telling a story that resonates with your audience and convinces them of your expertise. Here's a step-by-step guide to creating a compelling case study using The C.A.P.S.S. Technique.

Define Your Audience

Before you begin writing, identify who your case study is intended for. This step is crucial because understanding your audience will shape the language, tone, and focus of your case study. Are you targeting small business owners, corporate decision-makers, or professionals in a specific industry? The more you understand your audience's needs and pain points, the easier it will be to write a case study that resonates with them.

For example, if you're targeting manufacturers looking to improve their supply chain efficiency, your case study should focus on similar companies and highlight results that matter to that audience, like time savings, cost reductions, or improved logistics.

Present the Problem

Begin your case study by detailing the client's problem. This section should clearly explain the issue, the challenges faced, and the negative impact on the client. Be empathetic and relatable in your description to engage readers. The goal here is to ensure readers understand why the problem was significant and worthy of a solution.

Consider using storytelling techniques to draw readers into the situation. For instance, instead of just stating the problem, describe the frustration or inefficiency it caused for the client. This approach makes the case study more relatable and helps readers see themselves in the story.

Explain the Solution

The solution section should focus on how your product or service addressed the client's needs. This is your opportunity to showcase your expertise without coming across as overly promotional. Walk the reader through the steps you took to implement the solution, and be specific about the strategies or tools you used. This section is where you provide value by demonstrating how you solve problems effectively.

Be careful to avoid jargon or overly technical language unless your audience is familiar with such terms. Remember, the goal is to be informative, clear, and approachable. By focusing on how the solution unfolded, you build a narrative that is both educational and persuasive.

Showcase the Success

After presenting the solution, highlight the results. Quantifiable outcomes are ideal because they make the impact of your work tangible. Include metrics like increased revenue, reduced costs, or improved productivity. These numbers provide proof of success and reinforce your case study's credibility.

If specific numbers aren't available, you can still describe qualitative improvements, like enhanced customer satisfaction or streamlined operations. Readers need to feel confident that your solution worked, so present success stories in a way that is easy to grasp and leaves a strong impression.

This section is also where you can include any feedback or testimonials from the client, which can add a personal touch and reinforce your case study's credibility.

Include a Call to Action

The final part of your case study is the call to action. This should be a clear statement that encourages the reader to take the next step, whether contacting you, scheduling a consultation, or signing up for a newsletter. Make sure this invitation aligns with the goals of your case study. For example, if the case study focused on a consulting project, encourage readers to explore consulting services or set up an introductory call. It's important to create urgency with your call to action. Statistics show that your reader is more likely to reach out if you ask them to "Set Up an Introductory Call Now" as opposed to "Set Up an Introductory Call".

What Does a Good Case Study Look Like?

A successful case study is clear, well-organized, and speaks directly to the target audience. It should avoid unnecessary details and stay focused on the problem, solution, and success. Using The C.A.P.S.S. technique ensures each section has a clear purpose and flows logically. For example, a case study aimed at corporate clients should be formal and data-driven, while a case study for small businesses might be more conversational and include practical insights.

Ultimately, a good case study serves as a mirror for potential clients, helping them see themselves in the success story. By reading about another business's journey from problem to solution, readers gain confidence that your business can achieve similar results for them.

Case Study Examples and Their Impact

Case studies are versatile tools that can be tailored to fit various industries. Here are a few case study examples to illustrate how different sectors use this format:

- **Law Firms:** A law firm might create a case study around a landmark case, showing how they helped a client achieve a positive outcome. This can build trust among potential clients facing similar legal challenges.
- **Marketing Agencies:** A marketing agency may use a case study to demonstrate how it increased a client's brand visibility or engagement. This example would resonate with companies looking to improve their marketing efforts.
- **Medical Practitioners:** For a doctor or dentist, a case study might explore the effectiveness of a specific treatment for a client. This kind of case study can build trust with potential clients by showing real-world applications of medical techniques.

Each example shows the flexibility of case studies across different fields, proving their value as a marketing tool. When used effectively, case studies help clients connect with your brand, making them more likely to trust and engage with your business.

The Power of The C.A.P.S.S. Technique

An excellent case study or testimonial is more than just a story; it's a trust-building tool that shows clients how you have solved real-world problems. By following The C.A.P.S.S. technique and structuring your case studies and testimonials carefully, you can create a narrative that resonates with your audience and builds credibility. Remember, the goal is not just to present information but to persuade and encourage action.

Brand Elements

In the competitive world of small business, a strong, memorable brand is often the difference between standing out and blending in. Brand elements - like your logo, branding guidelines, photographs, and videos - are the visual and emotional cornerstones of your business identity. These are not just design components; they're powerful tools that shape how customers perceive your company and remember it over time. In a marketplace filled with choices, cohesive and high-quality brand elements provide small businesses with a unique opportunity to capture attention and build trust.

Your logo, for example, is often the first impression a customer has of your business. A high-resolution, professional logo can make your business look polished and credible across various media. Consistent branding guidelines go a step further, establishing a unified look and feel that reinforces your brand's identity every time it appears. When you add genuine, high-quality photographs and videos to the mix, you bring your brand to life in a way that resonates with customers, telling a story that's authentic and relatable.

This chapter dives into these essential brand elements, explaining why each plays a critical role in building brand loyalty and setting your small business apart from the competition. With the right approach, these elements don't just support your brand - they make it unforgettable.

Logo

Ensure your logo is a high-resolution vector image. This will make it versatile, capable of being used across various media without losing quality. A well-designed logo helps build brand recognition.

Consider using a service like 99 Designs to create your logo so you can get a wide variety of options at a reasonable price.

Branding Guidelines

Define your brand's core elements - color palette, fonts, and tone of voice - to create consistency. These guidelines ensure that every visual element reflects your brand's personality.

An online tool like Coolors is a fantastic and free way to create your company's color palette.

Photographs

High-quality images of your team, products, and workspace create a connection with visitors. Real photos (not stock images) often build more trust. Consider hiring a professional photographer for staff and office pictures.

Videos

Video content such as brand introductions or customer testimonials engages visitors. Quality videos can help tell your brand's story and demonstrate your value.

Website

In today's digital landscape, a business website is a powerful tool that enables brands to connect with customers, showcase their services, and gain credibility. This guide will show you how to build a business website, from gathering essential assets to ongoing maintenance. Following this roadmap will help you avoid common pitfalls and create a professional site that achieves your business goals.

Step 1: Gather Essential Assets

To start, gather all the assets needed to develop your brand identity and give your website a consistent look. These assets will play a major role in establishing trust with visitors and ensuring a unified brand experience. We recommend building your website with WordPress.

- **Website Hosting:** Choose a reliable web hosting provider like WPEngine for fast load times, robust security, and dependable support.
- **WordPress Theme:** Purchase a versatile theme like Divi from Elegant Themes, which offers design flexibility and a range of pre-built layouts.
- **Development Environment:** Set up a development environment where you can test site changes before going live. This helps prevent potential issues on the live site.

Step 2: Plan the Site

Planning your website ensures it aligns with your business goals and meets your audience's needs. This step involves defining your core message, organizing the site structure, and visualizing key pages.

Define the Message: Your website should reflect a clear message that resonates with your target audience. Define who they are, their demographics, and the problems your business solves. Categorize problems into three types: external (visible issues), internal (emotional concerns), and philosophical (your values or stance). Develop a solution plan that demonstrates how your offerings meet these needs, and add proof elements, like testimonials, awards, case studies, and success metrics, to build credibility. Be sure to state the promises you make to your clients (such as, "we return all calls within 1 business day"). Clearly state the success the client should expect if they work with you - or what failure looks like if they don't. Finally, bring it all home with an enticing and urgent Call to Action.

Sitemap Creation: Outline all main pages (e.g., Home, About, Services) and any additional pages, like a FAQ or Blog, for comprehensive site navigation. Don't forget legal pages, such as Terms of Service and Privacy Policy, as well as error pages and "Thank You" pages for post-interaction messaging. Be sure to perform keyword research using a tool like Ubersuggest and list the target keyword next to each page in the sitemap. This will help your site have excellent on-page SEO from launch.

Wireframe Key Pages: Create wireframes for pages that require unique layouts, like the Home page, service pages, or product landing pages. Wireframes are basic sketches that show where elements like text, images, and buttons should go. They're essential for a user-friendly and logical design structure.

Step 3: Design the Site

With your planning complete, it's time to bring your vision to life through design. Effective design combines aesthetics with functionality, helping visitors navigate your site and find the information they need.

Home Page Design Options: Develop two or three options for the Home page to explore different color schemes, and design styles. The Home page is often the first interaction visitors have with your brand, so it should be visually appealing and informative.

Key Page Designs: Once you've chosen a Home page design, move on to other key pages. You'll want to ensure that each page reinforces your brand's message while providing a smooth user experience. Consider up to two rounds of revisions to refine the design.

Photo/Video Shoot: If you haven't already gathered professional-quality photos and videos, now is the time. Investing in custom visuals makes your website more authentic and relatable.

Step 4: Code the Site

With your design assets and plan ready, it's time to start coding the website. This stage involves assembling your content, selecting images, and ensuring everything aligns with your brand's message.

Human-Edited AI Copy: AI tools can help generate content quickly and they're great at sticking to SEO best practices, but always have a human editor refine it to match your brand voice and ensure accuracy.

Edit Photos/Videos: Ensure that all images and videos are properly edited for lighting, color, content, and size. Optimized visuals improve page load speed, especially on mobile devices.

Select Final Imagery: Carefully choose images and videos that represent your brand and resonate with your audience. This is especially important on your Home page, where first impressions matter most.

Step 5: Launch the Site

Launching a site requires a meticulous quality control process to ensure a smooth experience for users. After all, your website serves as your online sales team, and any errors can impact credibility.

Final Quality Control Pass: Test all links and buttons. Confirm that each page is optimized for desktop, tablet, and mobile devices.

Connect Analytics Tools: Install analytics tools to gather data on how visitors interact with your site. This information will be valuable for future optimizations and tracking your return on investment (ROI).

Test Forms: Ensure all contact forms work correctly and that entries are saved and sent to the appropriate email addresses.

Launch: Once you've completed these steps, it's time to go live! Share the website with your network and celebrate your accomplishment.

Step 6: Ongoing Maintenance and Monitoring

A successful website requires regular maintenance. This final step will keep your site secure, up-to-date, and effective over time.

Hacker Protection: Keep plugins and themes updated to reduce vulnerabilities. Make nightly backups, so you can quickly restore your site if needed.

Uptime Monitoring: Use tools to ensure your website is consistently available. If your site goes down, uptime alerts will help you resolve the issue promptly.

Speed Optimization: Compress images and code, and cache pages. Page load speed is important for both SEO and user experience.

Content Updates: Regularly update your blog and replace outdated content. Fresh, relevant content keeps your audience engaged and enhances SEO.

How Much Does It Cost to Build a Business Website?

The cost of building a business website varies widely depending on its complexity and the resources you use. For a simple site using a DIY website builder, like Squarespace or Wix, the cost might be as low as $300 annually. However, if you're hiring a professional designer or agency, expect costs from $5,000 to $20,000 or more, depending on features, custom design, and additional integrations. Be wary of cheap website pitfalls, as opting for the cheapest option often leads to a lackluster design, poor functionality, and limited scalability.

Who Builds Websites?

You have several options when it comes to building your website:

Freelancers: Freelancers often provide custom design and development services at a lower cost than agencies. This is a good option if you have a clear vision but need a professional to execute it.

Web Design Agencies: Agencies offer a team of experts to handle design, development, and SEO. This option is generally the most expensive but ensures comprehensive service and support.

DIY Website Builders: For a more affordable route, use platforms like Wix or Squarespace. These tools offer templates and require no coding, making them ideal for smaller budgets or those who want to control the process. However, if you're new to the process you might find yourself quickly overwhelmed. Remember, your time is valuable - don't waste it learning a skill you'll only need once.

What Should a Business Website Do?

Your business website should do more than just present information; it should engage users, provide value, and encourage action. Here are the primary functions it should accomplish:

Establish Credibility: Showcase your expertise and build trust through testimonials, case studies, and industry awards.

Communicate Your Unique Value: Use concise, persuasive messaging to explain why visitors should choose you over competitors.

Make User Interaction Easy: Whether it's booking an appointment or purchasing a product, make it simple for users to complete the action.

Optimize for Mobile and SEO: Ensure your site is mobile-friendly and optimized for search engines to improve visibility and accessibility.

Is It Worth Making a Website for a Small Business?

Yes, building a website is one of the most valuable investments for a small business. A well-designed website establishes credibility, attracts new customers, and provides a way to showcase your products or services to a broader audience. Furthermore, with people increasingly searching online, not having a website can make your business appear outdated or less trustworthy. Building an effective website will enable you to reach potential customers beyond your immediate area, giving your small business a competitive edge.

No need to worry about complexity! Many small businesses thrive with just a simple one-page website. As long as it looks polished and clearly shares what you offer, you're all set!

With these steps, you now have a comprehensive guide on how to create a business website that's both effective and professional. From defining your brand to launching and maintaining the site, each step contributes to creating a strong online presence for your business.

Local Business Listings

Local business listings are essential tools for enhancing a business's online presence. These listings include vital business information - name, address, phone number (NAP), website, hours, and more - across various digital platforms. When customers search for services in a specific area, these listings help direct them to relevant businesses nearby. Common platforms for local listings include Google Business Profiles, Yelp, Bing Places, and Facebook Business.

In addition to attracting potential customers, well-maintained listings help establish a business's credibility. Properly managing these profiles across multiple platforms requires attention and consistency, which can be streamlined through local business listing management tools. These tools offer centralized control, making it easier to update information across all platforms simultaneously.

Are Local Business Listings a Scam?

Legitimate local business listings can significantly benefit businesses, connecting them to local customers and improving search engine rankings. However, there are scams to watch out for. Some services offer to "boost" a business's listing for a fee. In reality, paying for such services often leads to disappointment and even damages a business's online reputation. When a business pays for listing "boosts" on questionable platforms, there's a risk that positive customer reviews will be suppressed while negative reviews remain visible. This tactic pressures businesses to continue paying in hopes of maintaining a positive listing, creating a vicious cycle. Yelp and the Better Business Bureau are notorious for doing this to keep their subscriber numbers high.

Remember, you can access valuable visibility without fees. Exercise caution and avoid any service that charges recurring fees to "maintain" or "improve" your listing. Instead, focus on maintaining the quality of your free listing to protect your business's reputation.

Is Yelp a Scam?

Yelp is a legitimate and widely used platform for customer reviews. It has helped many businesses connect with local customers through detailed reviews, photos, and ratings. However, some businesses express concerns about Yelp's practices around paid advertising. There are reports that Yelp may prioritize businesses that pay for sponsored listings, while non-paying businesses find it harder to gain visibility.

One common complaint involves Yelp's review filtering system. Business owners sometimes feel that positive reviews are suppressed, while negative ones are prominently displayed. It's important to know that, regardless of any promotional offers from Yelp, businesses should not pay for services intended to manipulate listing performance. Instead, use Yelp's free business tools to manage reviews and respond to customer feedback in a way that builds trust. Paying for "review boosts" can lead to the perception that Yelp has control over review visibility, potentially harming your business's reputation in the long run.

How to Claim Your Google Business Profile Listing

Google Business Profiles is one of the most valuable tools for local businesses. Google's platform lets businesses appear on Google Search and Google Maps with verified information, making it easy for customers to find and contact them. To claim and optimize your Google Business Profile:

- Visit Google Business Profiles and sign in with your Google account.
- Search for your business name to check if it's already listed. If found, select it; if not, click on "Add your business to Google."
- Complete your business details, including name, address, phone number, hours, and category.
- Verify your business through mail, phone, or email, following Google's instructions.
- Once verified, regularly update your listing to include accurate hours, new photos, and recent promotions. Engaging with customer reviews is key to building trust and visibility on this platform.

How to Claim Your Yelp Listing

Yelp can provide a powerful local presence by displaying customer reviews and business details. Here's how to claim your Yelp listing:

- Visit the Yelp for Business page and log in or create a Yelp account.
- Search for your business on Yelp. If it already exists, select it; if not, you'll have the option to add it.
- Follow the prompts to verify ownership through email or phone. Yelp may require proof of association with the business.
- Once verified, you can manage your business information, update photos, and respond to reviews.

While Yelp may offer advertising options, carefully evaluate the terms and avoid paying for enhanced listing visibility. As with other platforms, paying for listings can lead to the perception that Yelp controls review visibility in a way that pressures businesses to continue paying for better results.

How to Claim Your Bing Places Listing

Bing Places is Microsoft's platform for local business listings, allowing businesses to appear in Bing search results. To claim your Bing Places listing:

- Go to Bing Places and sign in with your Microsoft account.
- Search for your business. If it's not already listed, click on "Add New Business."
- Provide your business details, including name, location, phone number, and hours.
- Verify your business via mail or phone, following Bing's instructions.
- Update your listing regularly to ensure accurate information for Bing users.

Like Google, Bing provides this listing service at no cost. Avoid any third-party offers to "boost" your Bing Places listing for a fee, as these often yield little benefit and can trap your business in recurring costs.

How to Set Up Your Facebook Business Listing

With over 2 billion users, Facebook offers an extensive platform for businesses to connect with customers through business listings, posts, and messaging. To set up your Facebook business listing:

- Log into your personal Facebook account and navigate to the Facebook Business Page creation page.
- Select "Business or Brand" as your page type and enter your business name and category.
- Fill in your contact information, including address, phone number, and website.
- Follow the prompts to complete the setup, add photos, and provide a detailed "About" section.
- Once your page is active, post updates, respond to customer messages, and monitor your page's performance through Facebook Insights.

Exploring Other Specialized Directories

In addition to popular platforms, specialized directories such as Super Lawyers, the Better Business Bureau, and Clutch can be advantageous for specific industries.

Super Lawyers is a popular listing service for legal professionals.

A Better Business Bureau (BBB) listing is a long-standing symbol of credibility. A BBB listing includes a review section where customers can leave ratings and comments. BBB charges fees for membership but it also allows you to claim a free listing with basic information.

Clutch is a specialized directory for business service providers that emphasizes client reviews and rankings. Businesses in fields like software development, consulting, and digital marketing benefit from a Clutch listing, as it provides industry-specific visibility.

Best Practices for Maintaining Local Business Listings

Successful local business listings require regular maintenance and engagement. Here are some best practices:

- **Keep Information Consistent:** Ensure your business name, address, phone number, and hours are consistent across all platforms. Consistency improves your credibility with both customers and search engines.
- **Engage with Customers:** Respond to customer reviews and questions promptly, whether they're positive or negative. Addressing feedback shows potential customers that you care about their experiences.
- **Add and Update Images**: Photos are essential for creating an attractive and engaging listing. Add high-quality images that showcase your products, services, and overall business environment. Refresh images periodically to keep your listing current, and consider including seasonal photos or updates that reflect recent changes.
- **Include Videos When Possible**: Videos can provide a dynamic, immersive experience for potential customers. Short videos of your store layout, key products, or customer experiences can make your business stand out. Many platforms now allow video uploads, and incorporating these can boost customer interest.
- **Keep Hours of Operation Accurate:** Always ensure that your hours of operation are up-to-date, as inaccurate hours can lead to customer frustration. If you change your business hours seasonally or have specific hours for different days, make sure your listing reflects those changes promptly.
- **Use Descriptive and Engaging Copy**: Most platforms allow a business description or summary. Make sure this description highlights your unique selling points and any current promotions or changes to your services. Update the description periodically to reflect seasonal offerings or new products.

By regularly managing these elements, you can improve customer engagement, and maintain an accurate, professional image online.

Holiday Hours and Special Updates

In addition to standard hours, it's essential to plan for adjustments during holidays and special events. Here's how to manage these updates effectively:

- **Holiday Hours**: Many platforms, including Google Business Profiles and Facebook, allow you to add holiday hours or mark special closures. Updating your listing with holiday hours prevents confusion and shows customers that your listing is accurate and reliable. Add these special hours well in advance of the holiday to ensure customers know when they can visit.
- **Special Events and Announcements**: If you host special events (like seasonal sales or customer appreciation days), use your listing to promote them. Platforms such as Google and Facebook allow for event announcements, which can attract more attention to your business.
- **Temporary Changes**: Sometimes, businesses need to temporarily adjust hours or services, such as during renovations or community events. Make sure these temporary changes are reflected in your listings to keep customers informed. Update your listing as soon as regular hours resume to maintain consistency.

By being proactive with updates, you ensure that your listing remains a reliable resource for customers, reducing confusion and enhancing their experience with your business.

Responding to Positive (and Negative) Customer Reviews

Customer reviews play a significant role in shaping your business's online reputation. Here are some best practices for handling both positive and negative feedback:

- **Responding to Positive Reviews**: Always acknowledge positive reviews to show appreciation. Thank the customer by name if possible, and mention a specific detail from their review if appropriate (e.g., "We're so glad you loved our coffee and cozy space!"). This makes your response feel personal and sincere. Additionally, use positive reviews as an opportunity to subtly encourage repeat visits or recommend other products.
- **Responding to Negative Reviews**: Negative reviews should be handled with care. Begin by acknowledging the customer's concern and apologizing for any inconvenience. Avoid sounding defensive, and keep your tone calm and understanding. If possible, offer a solution or invite the customer to reach out directly to resolve the issue privately. This shows others that you value feedback and are committed to improving customer satisfaction.
- **Stay Professional and Prompt**: Timely responses, ideally within a day or two, demonstrate that you are actively engaged with customer feedback. Remember that your responses to reviews are public, so always maintain a professional and friendly tone, even with critical feedback. Responding promptly to both positive and negative reviews reinforces trust and shows that you are attentive to customer experiences.

Final Thoughts

Local business listings are powerful resources for increasing visibility, attracting customers, and building credibility. By following the steps outlined here, you can effectively claim and manage listings across essential platforms like Google Business Profiles, Yelp, Bing Places listing, and Facebook business listing. Furthermore, specialized directories like Super Lawyers, Better Business Bureau, and Clutch can provide additional exposure for businesses in niche markets.

As a final note, be cautious with any service that charges to boost listings or manipulate reviews. Relying on trusted platforms and maintaining genuine customer relationships will lead to long-term benefits, helping your business establish a reputable and sustainable online presence.

The Digital Marketing Engine

Business owners who want to invest in marketing face a unique challenge. They have all of the relevant information and knowledge to generate more business, but lack the time and resources to share their story with the world. These techniques will show you how to share your knowledge in the most efficient way possible. The result will be more interest in your business and more leads.

Paid Media

For small businesses aiming to compete in today's digital world, paid media advertising (I'm going to refer to it as PPC or pay-per-click for the rest of this section) offers a way to reach specific audiences and boost traffic with a focused budget. However, to see a return on investment (ROI), understanding the options and strategies behind effective PPC campaigns is essential. This section explores the fundamentals of PPC, provides setup steps for popular platforms, and answers common questions to help you make informed decisions.

What Are Pay-Per-Click Ads?

PPC ads, short for Pay-Per-Click advertising, are paid online advertisements where businesses pay only when someone clicks on their ad. They're widely used on search engines like Google and social platforms such as Facebook to target specific keywords or user demographics. By paying per click, small businesses gain flexibility in their ad spend and can tailor ads to reach customers actively searching for related services or products.

PPC offers multiple advantages for small businesses: it provides measurable results, allows precise targeting, and enables businesses to quickly build visibility without a large upfront investment. However, PPC campaigns require careful setup, ongoing monitoring, and optimization to be cost-effective.

How Much Does PPC Cost Per Month?

The monthly cost of PPC varies depending on factors like industry, competition, and ad platform. For small businesses, typical PPC budgets range from $500 to $5,000 monthly. The most significant cost factors include:

- **Keyword Competition:** Higher competition keywords generally have higher costs per click.
- **Ad Platform:** Google Ads may cost more than Bing Ads due to user volume, but Bing's lower competition can make it a cost-effective choice for some businesses.
- **Ad Format:** Display ads and video ads may have different pricing models than search ads.

Effective small business PPC management involves setting a clear budget and tracking performance closely. This helps avoid overspending while focusing on ads that deliver results. Some platforms offer built-in budgeting tools to set daily limits, making it easier to manage monthly costs.

Is PPC Still Worth It?

For small businesses, PPC remains a valuable digital marketing tool. Unlike SEO, which may take months to show results, PPC offers near-instant visibility. Here's why PPC is worth considering:

- **Targeted Advertising:** Reach users by location, interests, demographics, and behavior.
- **Scalable Budgeting:** Adjust your budget anytime based on performance.
- **Fast Results:** Drive traffic and leads quickly, ideal for time-sensitive campaigns.

Tip: Focusing on the right forms of PPC can make a difference in results.

SEO vs. PPC for Small Businesses

SEO and PPC are the two most popular strategies for driving online traffic:

- **SEO (Search Engine Optimization):** SEO involves optimizing a website to rank higher on search engines like Google for relevant keywords. Although it takes time, SEO can yield lasting, organic traffic without continuous ad spend.
- **PPC:** With PPC, you pay for instant visibility. It's a great way to drive traffic immediately but requires ongoing budget allocation to maintain ad placement.

For small businesses, combining SEO with PPC creates a balanced approach. PPC can drive initial traffic while SEO gradually builds organic reach, allowing businesses to reduce reliance on paid ads over time.

What is Cost Per Click?

Cost Per Click (CPC) is the amount paid each time someone clicks on an ad. CPC rates depend on various factors:

- **Keyword Bids:** Higher bids can increase ad visibility but raise CPC.
- **Quality Score:** Ads with higher relevance and quality scores may achieve lower CPCs.
- **Competition:** Industries with many advertisers may have higher CPC rates.

Understanding CPC is essential for budgeting, as small businesses can control ad costs by adjusting keyword bids and refining targeting to attract relevant clicks without overspending.

What is Cost Per Impression?

Cost Per Impression (CPM) refers to the cost of 1,000 ad views, or "impressions." CPM is commonly used for display and video ads. For small businesses, CPM-based ads can be valuable for brand awareness campaigns, where increasing visibility matters more than direct clicks.

What is Branded PPC?

Branded PPC involves bidding on your business's name or product-specific keywords to capture search traffic directly related to your brand. For small businesses, branded PPC is beneficial because it:

- **Protects Brand Traffic:** Prevents competitors from capturing potential customers. Typically, if you can prove it's your brand you'll receive a steep discount over your competition on the ads.
- **Boosts Brand Visibility:** Ensures that customers find you first in search results.

Investing in branded PPC allows small businesses to secure their own search traffic, reducing the risk of losing customers to competitors who might bid on your brand terms.

How to Set Up Google Ads

Google Ads is one of the most popular PPC platforms. Here's how to set up a campaign:

1. **Create a Google Ads Account:** Access the dashboard to begin creating a campaign.
2. **Select Campaign Goal:** Choose a goal, such as sales, leads, or website traffic.
3. **Set Keywords and Bids:** Choose keywords related to your business and set bids based on your budget.
4. **Create Ad Content:** Write compelling ad copy and use visuals if applicable.

Google's remarketing options are particularly beneficial for small businesses, allowing them to target users who have interacted with their website previously.

How to Set Up Facebook Ads

Setting up Facebook ads involves accessing Facebook's Ads Manager and following these steps:

1. **Select Campaign Objective:** Choose an objective, such as awareness, consideration, or conversion, based on your goals.
2. **Define Audience:** Set parameters for location, demographics, interests, and behaviors.
3. **Budget and Schedule:** Choose a daily or lifetime budget, then set start and end dates.
4. **Create Ad Content:** Use engaging visuals and copy to capture attention and encourage clicks.

Facebook also supports Meta retargeting ads, allowing businesses to re-engage users who have previously interacted with their content. This option is particularly valuable for conversion-oriented campaigns.

How to Set Up Instagram Ads

Instagram ads run through Facebook's Ads Manager as well. Follow these steps to set up Instagram ads:

1. **Objective and Budget:** Select an objective and set your daily or lifetime budget.
2. **Define Target Audience:** Use Instagram's targeting features to reach specific groups.
3. **Choose Ad Format:** Choose from carousel ads, story ads, video ads, and more.
4. **Design Your Ad:** Use high-quality visuals and attention-grabbing text suited to Instagram's aesthetic.

Instagram's visually-driven platform is ideal for showcasing products and building brand identity. Leveraging Meta remarketing ads on Instagram can help convert users who have already shown interest in your business.

How to Set Up LinkedIn Ads

LinkedIn ads provide a platform for B2B marketing. Here's how to set up LinkedIn ads:

1. **Access Campaign Manager:** Create a new campaign from the LinkedIn Ads dashboard.
2. **Target Audience:** Define your audience based on job title, industry, or company size.
3. **Choose Ad Format:** Options include Sponsored Content, Message Ads, and Text Ads.
4. **Set Budget and Bids:** LinkedIn offers CPC and CPM options to help you manage spending.

LinkedIn ads are ideal for reaching decision-makers and professionals, making it a valuable channel for B2B small businesses.

How to Set Up Bing Ads

Bing ads offer lower competition than Google, making them a cost-effective option for small businesses. To set up Bing ads:

1. **Sign Up for Microsoft Advertising:** Create an account and access the campaign manager.
2. **Select Keywords:** Choose relevant keywords based on search volume and competition.
3. **Set Budget and Bids:** Bing allows you to set daily budgets and choose bidding options.
4. **Create Ads:** Write ad copy and upload visuals if needed.

With Bing's lower competition and strong demographic reach, it's an effective PPC platform for small businesses looking for high ROI.

How to Set Up Amazon Ads

Amazon ads target users already in buying mode, making them highly effective for product-based businesses. Here's how to set up Amazon ads:

1. **Create an Amazon Seller Central Account:** Access the Advertising Console from your dashboard.
2. **Select Campaign Type:** Choose between Sponsored Products, Sponsored Brands, and Sponsored Display.
3. **Set Bids:** Choose bid amounts for keywords to control visibility and costs.
4. **Optimize Keywords:** Use keywords related to your product to reach relevant customers.

Amazon ads are a powerful option for product visibility, but they work best with well-optimized listings and relevant keywords.

How to Set Up Google Product Listing Ads

Google Product Listing Ads (PLAs), also known as Shopping ads, are a powerful tool for ecommerce businesses to showcase their products directly on Google's search results pages. These ads display product images, titles, prices, and the business name, making it easy for potential customers to find and buy your products. Here's a step-by-step guide to setting up Google Product Listing Ads:

1. **Set Up a Google Merchant Center Account:** Start by creating an account on Google Merchant Center. This platform allows you to upload and manage your product inventory for Google Shopping ads. Be sure to fill out your business information accurately and follow Google's guidelines to avoid any issues with your account.
2. **Upload Your Product Feed:** Google requires a product feed, a file that contains detailed information about each product, such as title, description, price, availability, and image links. You can create this feed manually or by exporting data from your ecommerce platform. Once your feed is ready, upload it to your Google Merchant Center account, either manually or by setting up automatic updates if you make frequent product changes.
3. **Verify and Claim Your Website:** Google requires you to verify that you own the website associated with your product listings. In the Google Merchant Center, navigate to "Business information," then "Website," and follow the instructions to verify and claim your website. This step is essential to link your site with Google Ads and display your products effectively.
4. **Link Google Ads and Google Merchant Center Accounts:** To create Product Listing Ads, you'll need to link your Google Merchant Center account with your Google Ads account. In the Merchant Center, go to "Settings," then "Linked Accounts," and choose Google Ads. This linkage allows Google to use the product data from your Merchant Center for your ad campaigns.
5. **Create a Shopping Campaign in Google Ads:** Now, log in to your Google Ads account and create a new campaign. Select "Shopping" as the campaign type, then choose "Sales" or "Website traffic" as your goal. Select

the Merchant Center account you linked and choose your target country, which determines where your ads will appear.

6. **Configure Your Campaign Settings:** In the campaign setup, specify your daily budget, bidding strategy, and location targeting. You can choose between standard and smart Shopping campaigns. Standard campaigns offer more control, allowing you to adjust bids and targeting, while smart campaigns use Google's machine learning to optimize ad placement and bids for you.

7. **Organize Product Groups:** Google Shopping campaigns use product groups to organize your inventory. By default, Google places all your products in one group. However, to improve performance, consider dividing products into smaller groups based on categories, price range, or other relevant factors. This setup enables you to set different bids for various product types, optimizing your ad spend.

8. **Optimize Bids and Monitor Performance:** Set initial bids based on your budget and adjust them as you gather performance data. Monitor key metrics like impressions, clicks, and conversions to determine which products perform well and which need improvement. Regularly optimizing bids based on performance helps maximize your return on investment.

9. **Maintain Your Product Feed:** Google requires up-to-date and accurate product information. Regularly update your feed to reflect changes in price, stock, and availability, and ensure your images and descriptions meet Google's requirements. A well-maintained product feed can improve ad relevance and overall performance.

Setting up Google Product Listing Ads takes time, but the potential reach and visual impact make it worthwhile. These ads allow customers to see your products upfront, making them more likely to click and convert. By following these steps, you can create effective Google Shopping campaigns that drive sales and visibility for your products.

What Are Retargeting Ads?

Retargeting ads are designed to reach users who have visited your website or social media but didn't convert. By displaying relevant ads, you can re-engage these users and encourage conversions. Retargeting ads are valuable for small businesses aiming to maximize ROI.

What is Remarketing?

Remarketing refers to re-engaging users through follow-up marketing, often via email. By targeting users who have previously interacted with your brand, remarketing helps improve brand recall and can lead to higher conversion rates.

The Difference Between Retargeting and Remarketing

While both methods aim to re-engage previous visitors, retargeting typically refers to ad placements on social media or search engines, while remarketing often uses email campaigns or targeted follow-ups.

Recommended PPC Types for Small Businesses

When it comes to choosing PPC options that deliver strong ROI for small businesses, focusing on the right platforms and ad formats is crucial. Not all PPC methods work equally well for smaller budgets or niche markets, which is why you should prioritize the following PPC types:

- **Branded Ads:** Bidding on keywords specific to your brand or products helps ensure that customers find your business first when they search for your brand name. This strategy is effective for capturing brand-specific traffic and preventing competitors from appearing above you in search results. Branded ads are particularly valuable for businesses with high brand recognition or unique offerings that may attract competitive interest.
- **Google Retargeting Ads:** Google retargeting ads target users who have already visited your website, keeping your brand top of mind as they browse other websites or platforms. This type of ad improves conversion rates by reaching people already familiar with your business, often guiding them to complete a purchase or revisit your site. Banner images and video ads work great here.
- **Meta Retargeting Ads (Facebook & Instagram):** Meta retargeting ads on Facebook and Instagram use advanced data and user behavior insights to serve ads to users based on their previous actions. By targeting those who have already shown interest in your business, these ads allow small businesses to drive engagement and conversions in a cost-effective way.
- **Bing Ads:** Although often overlooked, Bing ads offer a powerful platform for small businesses. Bing users tend to be slightly older, have higher incomes, and convert well, making Bing ads highly cost-effective for small business advertisers. Additionally, with less competition than Google, Bing ads can deliver a strong ROI while still reaching a wide audience, especially in certain demographics.

By concentrating on these PPC types, small businesses can make the most of their advertising budgets. Each of these recommended options allows for precise targeting, a focus on re-engagement, and a high likelihood of conversion, making them optimal choices for small businesses looking to grow their digital footprint.

Conclusion

PPC advertising offers small businesses an effective way to gain visibility, drive traffic, and increase conversions with a focused approach. However, choosing the right PPC options is essential to maximizing return on investment. By prioritizing branded ads and retargeting through platforms like Google, Meta, and Bing, small businesses can reach the audiences most likely to engage with their brand and complete purchases. With careful budgeting, targeted campaigns, and a focus on re-engaging warm leads, small businesses can make PPC a powerful part of their marketing strategy. As you implement these strategies, remember to monitor performance metrics closely, adjust your bids and budgets as needed, and continually optimize for the best results. In today's competitive digital landscape, these PPC recommendations can help small businesses thrive and achieve sustainable growth.

Content Repurposing

Content repurposing provides a rare opportunity by capturing your knowledge via video in a limited amount of time. In other words, **you get all the results of traditional marketing efforts, but with much less effort on your end**.

1. Research & Prep

Content repurposing starts with research. We want to get a general idea of where the fish are and where we want to put our net.

We consult a few fishing guides — in this case, Google's tools — to find out what the fish are biting on.

2. Expert Interview Videos

Once we know what the fish are biting on, we film a subject matter expert at the business (like the owner, a sales person, or an engineer) talking about that topic. And then we take that information and distribute it across as many different channels as possible to lay the net.

Channels include YouTube, which is the world's third-largest search engine. Or Google, which of course is the world's largest search engine. Or TikTok, which is the largest search engine for people under 30.

3. Distribution & Republication

With content repurposing your content will end up on YouTube in the form of a video. It will appear on Google in the form of a blog post on your website. It will show up as podcast episodes on Spotify, iTunes, and all the different places that people go for podcasts.

And then it's going to show up as videos, images, and captions across social media. Twitter/X, Facebook, LinkedIn, Instagram, and TikTok.

And finally, your content will be used to nurture your audience in the form of a monthly newsletter.

To sum up, these five outputs will be your fishing net:

1. Blog posts
2. Videos
3. Social media
4. Podcasts
5. Nurturing emails

With a great website in place, people will actually *want* to give you their contact information in exchange for a high-value PDF, checklist, etc.

What makes this marketing technique special is all five outputs only require one session with the subject matter expert. Again, the return on time investment is crucial, and this process is mindful of that. The return on investment for this process is massive. It's not a super bowl commercial. It's a low-risk marketing strategy.

Blog Posts

When it comes to blog posts, keyword research isn't just a task - it's a critical strategy. It defines how well your content connects with your audience and whether it appears where it matters: at the top of search results. This chapter dives deep into the art and science of keyword research, breaking it down into actionable steps to help you build a strong foundation for your SEO efforts.

You'll learn how to identify your target audience, leverage essential tools, and analyze the metrics that guide smart decision-making. Whether you're a seasoned marketer refining your process or a small business owner looking to gain a competitive edge, these insights will ensure your efforts drive meaningful, quality traffic to your site.

Understanding keyword research doesn't end with knowing what people are searching for; it's about grasping why they're searching and tailoring your content to align with their intentions. By the end of this chapter, you'll have a roadmap for identifying the right keywords, improving your search rankings, and crafting content that truly resonates with your audience.

Keyword Research

Keyword research forms the foundation of SEO, helping you understand your audience and create content that ranks well. This guide covers everything you need to know, including how to identify your target audience, which tools to use, and how to analyze key metrics. Let's dive into each step to ensure your keyword research efforts drive quality traffic to your site.

For our purposes the term "keyword" can denote either a single word or a complete phrase.

Understand Your Audience

Effective keyword research begins with a clear understanding of your target audience. Knowing who you're targeting and what they're interested in allows you to tailor content to meet their specific needs. For example, if your target audience is property managers, your approach should center on their unique challenges and information needs.

Clarify your audience's needs and intentions. By putting yourself in your audience's shoes, you can better understand what they might search for. Think like a property manager, rather than someone selling to them. This shift in perspective helps you identify their daily pain points and areas where they need information, enabling you to develop content that speaks directly to their concerns.

How to Define Your Audience

This is the same process as Step 2 of your website. For ease of reference: get to know your audience's demographics and the challenges your business can help solve. Think of these challenges in three categories: external (the obvious stuff), internal (the emotional side), and philosophical (their values and beliefs).

Conduct Prep Work and Deepen Your Audience Insights

Once you have a firm grasp of your audience, the next step is gathering deeper insights into their search behaviors. This step requires creativity. Instead of just looking at data analytics, immerse yourself in their world by exploring the types of questions they might ask online. Consider browsing forums, checking industry-related social media groups, or even examining popular blogs in your niche.

If, for example, you're focused on property managers, avoid viewing their questions only from a sales perspective. Instead, try to consider their informational needs, such as the average failure rate of different models of ovens - or a comparison of different tools used to track service calls, without the influence of sales-related objectives. By keeping your focus on pure information needs, you gain a clearer picture of what potential clients are genuinely interested in and what might motivate their searches.

Practical Ways to Learn About Your Audience

- Explore relevant industry job listings to understand their responsibilities
- Conduct online research with common industry queries
- Reach out to individuals within the target field for firsthand insights

Study Search Engine Results Pages (SERPs)

Understanding SERPs, the pages that show after a search, is critical in keyword research. Google prioritizes content similar to what's already ranking. Thus, you need to assess what is currently ranking for your target keywords to ensure your content aligns with search intent.

For instance, if you're trying to rank for "pie chart" in a baking context, you may find that the SERPs prioritize data visualization results rather than baked goods. In this case, Google would likely not rank your content highly, as it doesn't align with the search intent. Checking SERPs before creating content saves time and helps you avoid targeting keywords unlikely to succeed.

Determine Domain Authority

Domain Authority (DA) measures the strength of a website's backlink profile, among other factors, and indicates how well a site might rank in search results. Websites with higher DA scores tend to perform better in search engine rankings. To check DA, you can use free tools like the MozBar Chrome extension, which allows you to see DA directly on SERPs.

Alternatively, you can go straight to the source and use Moz's Domain Authority Checker.

A general rule of thumb is to target keywords with difficulty scores no more than 15 points above your site's DA. For example, if your DA is 20, avoid keywords with a difficulty score exceeding 35. Keeping within a feasible range helps you rank more effectively while preventing wasted effort on highly competitive terms.

Factors Affecting Domain Authority

- **Backlinks:** The quantity and quality of links pointing to your site
- **Engagement:** The amount of time users spend on your pages
- **Reputation:** Links from trustworthy sources

Utilize Keyword Research Tools

Keyword research tools can streamline the process and provide deeper insights. Below are two popular options that offer a variety of features:

- **Ubersuggest:** A free tool that offers essential keyword insights. Though it has some limitations in data speed and features, it's a solid choice for basic research. Just be sure to manually refresh your results to ensure they're up-to-date.
- **KWFinder:** A subscription-based tool that allows for detailed analysis and organization. KWFinder provides options to filter by location and language, making it ideal for geographically specific targeting. It also allows you to save keywords in lists for easy tracking.

Choose a tool that fits your needs, budget, and the level of detail you want. Both Ubersuggest and KWFinder are easy to use, and each offers unique strengths that can enhance your keyword research process.

If you want to go directly to the source, consider using Google Keyword Planner. This is the source of information that drives Ubersuggest and KWFinder (and other related tools). It might not be the easiest to use, but it's still a fantastic tool!

Analyze Key Metrics

When analyzing potential keywords, focus on the following key metrics:

Trend Analysis

Start by examining the trend line for your keywords. Keywords with stable or rising trends suggest ongoing interest, making them more reliable targets. Avoid keywords with a steep downward trend, as they may lose relevance over time.

Search Volume

Search volume measures the monthly search frequency for a given keyword. For niche industries, a minimum search volume of 100 per month can still be effective. For broader topics, aim for 1,000 or more. The ideal search volume varies by industry, so tailor this to your specific niche.

SEO Difficulty

SEO Difficulty measures the competitive landscape for a keyword. Lower scores indicate easier competition, while higher scores suggest more challenging targets. As mentioned, try to stay within a difficulty range no more than 15 points above your site's DA for the best chances of ranking.

Cost per Click (CPC)

While CPC is primarily for paid advertising, it also indicates keyword value. A CPC of $1 or more suggests that businesses find the keyword valuable enough to invest in, which can indicate buyer intent and signal that it's worth targeting in your organic efforts. High CPC keywords often have higher conversion potential.

Use Questions to Capture Long-Tail Traffic

Long-tail keywords, short phrases with three or more words used in an online search, can attract more specific, intent-driven traffic. Including common questions related to your main keyword can capture this traffic effectively. KWFinder's questions feature allows you to see what people are asking about a given topic.

For instance, if you're researching "key fob systems," you may find questions like "How much does a key fob system cost?" Including these questions in your content improves your chances of ranking for both the primary and related queries.

Ubersuggest also lists related questions when you search for a keyword.

Another way to find these questions is to type the keyword into Google and review the list of questions that comes up on the SERP.

Prioritize Short Keywords While Incorporating Long-Tail Queries

When performing keyword research, start with short keywords and add long-tail versions as subtopics. For example, targeting "key fob system" as your primary keyword still enables your content to rank for longer phrases containing this term.

While long-tail keywords can be highly specific, keeping your primary focus on shorter terms makes your content more versatile and helps capture a broader audience. Use questions and subtopics to incorporate longer terms without diluting your core focus.

Avoid Over-Reliance on Auto-Complete Suggestions

Some SEO practitioners use Google's auto-complete feature for keyword ideas. However, auto-complete results can be too broad or sometimes even irrelevant. Definitely keep them in mind, but try to rely on verified keyword tools to ensure accuracy and avoid filler content that may not bring valuable traffic to your site.

Conclusion

SEO keyword research is essential for building a successful SEO strategy. By understanding your audience, using effective tools, and analyzing key metrics, you can identify high-value keywords that attract relevant traffic to your site. Remember to balance short and long-tail keywords, check SERPs, and use tools like KWFinder and Ubersuggest to streamline your process.

With a strategic approach to keyword research, you'll be well-positioned to create content that resonates with your audience, ranks well, and drives sustainable traffic over time.

SEO vs. AI

In today's digital landscape, SEO and AI are reshaping how businesses optimize content for search engines, leading to a new era of enhanced, intelligent marketing. As artificial intelligence becomes integral to search engine optimization (SEO), businesses gain valuable tools for boosting search rankings, analyzing data, and optimizing content strategies. This section provides an in-depth look at the future of SEO and AI by answering key questions, helping business owners understand how AI impacts SEO and how to harness its potential.

How is AI Used in SEO?

AI has rapidly become a foundational element of modern SEO strategies. By analyzing massive amounts of data and identifying patterns, AI enhances multiple areas within SEO, from keyword research to content creation and technical optimization. At the core of a SEO and AI overview lies Google's algorithm, which continually adapts to provide the most relevant and valuable results. AI-driven SEO tools help marketers keep pace with these changes, enabling better data analysis and making it easier to adapt to the algorithm's nuances.

One major way AI contributes to SEO is through natural language processing (NLP). NLP allows search engines to better understand user queries, intent, and context. This understanding helps content creators match their material more closely with what users are looking for, ultimately improving rankings. AI also helps automate processes like on-page SEO auditing, identifying errors, and suggesting improvements. Through AI-powered tools, businesses can quickly pinpoint technical issues, optimize page structure, and ensure they meet SEO best practices.

Moreover, AI enables deeper personalization by analyzing user behavior. For instance, it can track how users interact with content, what they find engaging, and where they lose interest. This level of insight allows businesses to craft more targeted, effective content. AI's influence in SEO is particularly visible in tools that recommend content topics, predict keyword trends, and even generate suggestions for internal links to boost a page's visibility.

Is SEO Going to Be Replaced by AI?

While AI is an influential tool in SEO, it is unlikely to replace SEO altogether. SEO relies on human insights, creativity, and expertise to create authentic, engaging content that resonates with users. The fundamental purpose of SEO - to attract and retain users by delivering valuable information - remains unchanged. Content is king, and quality content will always play a critical role in achieving SEO success. No matter how advanced AI becomes, it cannot fully replicate the human touch in content creation.

AI augments SEO by simplifying data analysis, automating repetitive tasks, and providing valuable insights. However, it still requires human oversight to interpret data, create comprehensive strategies, and ensure content aligns with brand values and audience needs. While AI can generate SEO content, human judgment is essential to evaluate quality and relevance, fine-tune tone, and ensure compliance with Google's guidelines.

In the end, SEO and AI complement each other. Rather than one replacing the other, they work together to enhance overall marketing performance. AI empowers SEO experts to do their jobs more efficiently, but the need for skilled professionals to manage, guide, and innovate within SEO remains unchanged. So, while AI may redefine how we approach SEO, it will not replace SEO as a critical business function.

AI isn't a direct threat to SEO but is transforming traditional SEO practices. Historically, SEO focused heavily on keyword density and link building. However, with advanced AI algorithms, search engines are now more adept at recognizing high-quality content and distinguishing it from low-value, keyword-stuffed pages. This shift challenges SEO practitioners to produce better, more user-focused content.

The "threat" AI poses is mainly to outdated SEO practices. Search engines now prioritize content that provides real value, encouraging marketers to move beyond superficial optimization. The emphasis is on understanding user intent, a task that AI facilitates through algorithms capable of assessing whether content meets searcher expectations. For instance, AI algorithms can now analyze the context of a page to see if it genuinely addresses the topic, allowing for a more holistic view of content quality.

Embracing AI-driven SEO tools, businesses can ensure that their SEO and AI generated content remains relevant and meets modern search requirements. AI creates opportunities for SEO professionals to refine their strategies and shift their focus to user engagement and experience, turning AI from a perceived threat into an essential ally in maintaining SEO effectiveness.

Can AI Write SEO Content?

AI-driven tools, such as ChatGPT, have proven highly effective at generating content, including SEO content. However, the quality and effectiveness of AI-written content can vary. Tools like these draw from extensive data to create text based on user prompts, making it easier to produce content at scale. AI can quickly generate outlines, topic ideas, and even full articles optimized with relevant keywords, supporting content strategies by reducing the time spent on initial drafts.

However, AI-generated content often lacks the nuance and creativity that human writers provide. While AI can efficiently develop SEO and AI generated content, it tends to produce material that is straightforward but lacks depth. Effective SEO content requires expertise, especially to provide insights and unique perspectives that stand out. AI is a valuable tool for creating a foundation, but human input is essential for refining content to resonate with specific audiences, ensuring it addresses their needs. The best AI-generated SEO content uses a combination of unique, expert input prior to content generation alongside human edits to the AI output.

In other words, the ideal approach is to combine AI and human efforts. AI can generate initial drafts, handle keyword optimization, and structure content, while humans review and enhance it. This collaborative approach leverages AI's speed and data capabilities without sacrificing the quality and personalization that human writers bring to content creation.

Can SEO Detect AI?

With the proliferation of AI-generated content, search engines and SEO tools are developing methods to detect AI-driven material. These tools, known as SEO AI detectors, are designed to assess whether content has been created by AI, as search engines increasingly prioritize authenticity. Google's algorithm can detect patterns typical of AI-generated text, such as repetitive phrases or generic language that lacks specificity.

Using AI detection tools, marketers can verify that their content aligns with Google's quality standards, preventing penalties associated with low-quality or overly generic material. These tools offer valuable feedback, ensuring that even if AI is used for initial content generation, the final product meets the standards for quality and relevance. For businesses, this means maintaining a balance: leveraging AI for efficiency but upholding the authenticity that search engines value.

AI detectors play a vital role in maintaining content quality, providing a way to measure and adjust AI-generated content to avoid potential SEO pitfalls. By using these tools, businesses can protect their SEO strategy, ensuring their content remains competitive and search engine-friendly.

Does ChatGPT-Generated Text Hurt Your SEO?

ChatGPT and similar AI tools can be valuable resources for content creation, but they should be used carefully to avoid potential SEO risks. While AI-generated text does not inherently harm SEO, excessive reliance on it can lead to issues. If content is generic, repetitive, or fails to engage readers, search engines may penalize the page for low engagement.

SEO marketing relies on measuring return on investment. User engagement, such as time spent on a page and interactions, contributes positively to SEO. If ChatGPT-generated content does not meet user expectations, it may lead to high bounce rates, signaling to search engines that the page is not valuable. This can harm rankings over time.

Conclusion

The evolving relationship between SEO and AI presents both opportunities and responsibilities for business owners. As AI advances, it offers powerful tools that enhance SEO efforts, from generating content to analyzing user intent. However, successful SEO still requires human insight, creativity, and strategic oversight. By integrating SEO and generative AI tools, marketers can streamline processes, improve personalization, and stay competitive in the digital landscape.

In summary, the key to leveraging AI in SEO is balance. AI can provide efficiency, data-driven insights, and support for content creation, but the human ability to understand and connect with users remains irreplaceable. As businesses embrace the future of search engine optimization and AI, they should adopt AI-driven solutions while maintaining a focus on quality and relevance. By doing so, companies can secure a prominent place in search engine results, ensuring long-term visibility and success in an AI-enhanced digital world.

Writing a Blog with AI

Blogging is the act of creating and sharing written content online, often on a dedicated website or platform, with the purpose of informing, entertaining, or educating a specific audience. It started in the early days of the Internet as "weblogs," where users documented personal stories, thoughts, or ideas for others to read. Over time, blogging has transformed into a key part of content marketing, helping businesses build a loyal audience and enhance brand credibility by sharing relevant, helpful information.

Today, blogging is a core strategy in digital marketing. Businesses use it to improve visibility in search engines, connect with customers, and establish authority in their industry. However, creating quality blog content requires a strategic approach, not just in writing but in planning and structuring each post. This is where the Skyscraper Technique comes in, a method of crafting content by researching existing high-performing posts, enhancing them, and then producing a superior version. This method allows bloggers to maximize their reach by understanding what resonates with their target audience. You can use this technique to enhance your existing blogs (especially ones that show early signs of engagement). You can even use it to turn video transcripts or voice memos into high quality blog posts. The Skyscraper Technique has become even more valuable with the advent of consumer AI tools like ChatGPT.

To stay competitive, especially with the rise of AI in marketing, many companies leverage artificial intelligence to create and refine content. AI blogging software aids in identifying popular topics, predicting audience engagement, and even helping with content creation, which can significantly streamline the blogging process.

Can I Use AI for Blogging?

Absolutely. AI has introduced numerous tools and techniques that make blogging more efficient and effective. AI blogging tools help bloggers generate content ideas, outline topics, and even draft initial articles. These tools analyze data from existing content, track trends, and identify keywords that are relevant to your audience. As a result, bloggers can produce more targeted content in less time.

For example, AI-based tools like Ubersuggest allow bloggers to conduct detailed keyword research. You can type in a topic and see data on monthly search volume, keyword difficulty, and related terms. This information enables you to craft blog posts that are optimized for search engines, increasing your chances of ranking higher. By examining high-ranking posts on similar topics, you can employ the Skyscraper Technique to outline a blog that improves upon the competition by offering deeper insights, clearer information, and additional value.

AI blog writing also benefits from tools that suggest enhancements based on readability and engagement metrics. Some AI tools analyze content performance on various platforms, predicting the elements of a blog post that are likely to draw attention. By leveraging these insights, bloggers can tweak their content to keep readers engaged, resulting in longer session times and a higher likelihood of conversion. AI tools simplify these processes, making it easier to create effective content with a strong return on investment.

Will AI Replace Blogging?

AI will not replace blogging; instead, it will redefine the process by streamlining certain aspects. Human insight, creativity, and intuition remain essential for producing engaging content that resonates with readers. While AI blogging software can generate written content quickly and effectively, it lacks the ability to capture personal perspectives and nuanced storytelling, which are key to effective blogging.

The role of a blogger is shifting towards a hybrid position, blending content creation with strategic oversight. With AI handling much of the data analysis and optimization, bloggers can focus on crafting meaningful stories and unique content that resonates with readers on a human level. Think of AI as a tool that enhances the blogging process rather than a replacement. For instance, AI might

---

help you understand how to better structure a post, while you ensure the content maintains an authentic voice.

Consider the Skyscraper Technique: while AI can suggest improvements based on current high-ranking content, it takes a human touch to truly make it better. AI can provide a framework, but bloggers bring creativity and insight that AI lacks. Ultimately, AI empowers bloggers to make their content more effective without diminishing the importance of human expertise in creating memorable and relatable posts.

Are Blogs Becoming Obsolete?

While the digital landscape is constantly evolving, blogs are far from obsolete. In fact, blogs remain an essential part of digital marketing and SEO strategies for many businesses. Blogs are powerful tools for establishing authority, driving organic traffic, and nurturing customer relationships. Content like AI blog posts keeps brands relevant in search results, providing answers to common questions and insights that people are actively seeking online.

However, the approach to blogging has evolved. Today, simply writing and posting a blog isn't enough to attract an audience. With millions of new posts published daily, businesses need to prioritize quality and relevance to stand out. Tools like the Skyscraper Technique, combined with AI-driven insights, allow bloggers to create better content by identifying and improving upon popular topics. Blogs that follow these strategies see higher engagement rates, helping businesses stay visible and authoritative.

For example, if you're writing about "AI in marketing," use AI tools to research the top articles on this topic. Then, take those articles and create something even better. Blogs are not disappearing - they are adapting. By aligning content with user intent and ensuring it provides real value, bloggers keep their sites relevant and engaging.

Using AI to Write Blogs

Once you're satisfied with the results of your research you can use a tool like ChatGPT to outline or even write the blog post for you. Of course, it's critical for a human to review the AI-written blog post and adjust it to match the brand's voice and messaging guidelines. It's not common but sometimes AI tools will include details that contradict your company's opinion - so, you'll want to edit that content.

AI blogging tools are "garbage in, garbage out" - meaning, the quality of the results depends on your prompts. ChatGPT 4o has a feature called "memories" where you can provide up to 12 prompts that it will keep in mind as it crafts the post for you.

The following prompts are the most important:

1. Write a 1500 to 2000 word long article
2. Write the article in HTML markup
3. Include a heading every 250 to 400 words
4. Begin 30% to 40% of the sentences in the article with a transition word
5. Never use passive voice
6. Never use adverbs
7. Use normal blog post formatting, including headings and bullet points
8. Use the company's brand name
9. Target an audience within a specific demographic
10. Target a specific keyword and answer specific questions
11. Include additional specific keywords
12. Use a provided transcript from a video or voice memo or an existing blog post

Conclusion

In summary, AI blogging tools and the Skyscraper Technique enable content creators to elevate their blogging strategy, maximizing engagement, visibility, and authority. AI and SEO will continue to evolve, offering bloggers new ways to innovate and grow within the ever-changing digital landscape. With AI as a supportive tool, blogging becomes simpler and more effective, paving the way for content that truly stands out.

Videos

Video marketing combines compelling storytelling with strategic distribution to engage audiences, while recording videos remotely leverages modern tools and techniques to create professional-quality content from virtually anywhere.

Video Marketing

In today's fast-paced digital world, video for business marketing has become a critical tool for small businesses looking to grow. Whether you're trying to build your brand, drive traffic to your website, or convert viewers into loyal customers, video content offers a highly engaging way to connect with your audience. In this section, we'll cover everything you need to know about using video for business marketing, including setting up your YouTube channel, tracking key performance indicators (KPIs), creating high-quality videos, and more.

What is Video Marketing?

Video marketing refers to the process of using video content to promote your business, products, or services. For small businesses, video marketing can help establish a presence on platforms like YouTube and drive traffic to their websites. Video marketing allows companies to tell their stories in an engaging way, showcase their products, and build deeper connections with potential customers. When properly executed, video marketing can significantly increase brand awareness and conversions.

Why Use Video for Business Marketing?

The benefits of video for business marketing go beyond simply sharing information. Videos can engage your audience in ways that text and images alone cannot. Here are a few key reasons why small businesses should incorporate video into their marketing strategies:

- **Higher engagement:** Video content grabs attention and holds it longer than written content, making it more effective for delivering your message.
- **Improved SEO:** Search engines prioritize video content, especially from platforms like YouTube, which can help improve your website's search rankings.
- **Increased conversions:** Videos can explain your product or service more clearly, leading to better conversion rates.
- **Stronger brand connection:** Videos provide a personal touch, allowing customers to connect with your brand on an emotional level.

When you combine these benefits with the wide reach of platforms like YouTube, video for business marketing becomes one of the most powerful tools in your marketing arsenal.

How to Measure Success with Video Marketing

Key Performance Indicators (KPIs)

Before diving into video creation, it's crucial to understand how to measure the success of your video for business marketing efforts. Key performance indicators (KPIs) help you track whether your videos are achieving your business goals. For YouTube, focus on three simple KPIs:

- **Likes:** Although small businesses may not accumulate tons of likes, this metric serves as a leading indicator of how well your video resonates with viewers.
- **Video watch time:** This KPI indicates how long viewers engage with your content. The longer people watch, the better your video content connects with the audience.
- **Clickthrough rate:** This measures how many viewers click from your video to your website. It's essential to have Google Analytics set up to track these clicks and determine whether your videos are driving traffic and conversions.

Tracking these KPIs allows you to make data-driven decisions that will enhance your video marketing strategy over time.

Why is Video Marketing Important?

For small businesses, video marketing is more than just a trend. It's a crucial part of staying competitive in the digital landscape. As consumer behavior shifts more toward video content, businesses that fail to leverage video risk falling behind. Video marketing not only captures attention but also enhances trust and credibility with your audience. When done well, it can turn casual viewers into loyal customers.

Video marketing is important for several reasons:

- **Better communication:** Video simplifies complex ideas and makes your message more accessible to a broader audience.
- **Higher retention:** Viewers are more likely to remember your message when it's delivered through a video than through text or images alone.
- **Social media engagement:** Videos are highly shareable, and platforms like Facebook, Instagram, and LinkedIn prioritize video content.
- **Build trust:** Video content creates a personal connection with your audience, making your brand feel more approachable.
- **Improve conversion rates:** Including videos on your website or landing pages can increase conversion rates by as much as 80%.
- **Reach a wider audience:** Videos are more likely to be shared, expanding your reach organically.

Creating High-Quality Videos for Your Business

Now that you understand the importance of video for business marketing, let's explore how to create high-quality videos without breaking the bank. For small business owners, production value is important, but it doesn't need to be overwhelming. Here are some essential tips:

1. Plan Your Video Content

Before you start filming, outline what you want to achieve with your video. Are you introducing a new product, demonstrating a service, or building brand awareness? Defining your goal will help you craft a clear message. And be sure to craft that message from the perspective of the viewer. They'll be more engaged if you're telling their story instead of your company's.

2. Invest in Basic Equipment

You don't need to spend a fortune on video equipment. Many modern smartphones, like iPhones and Androids, shoot in 4K quality. Use a tripod to stabilize your camera, and invest in a simple ring light for better lighting. Good lighting can dramatically improve the quality of your video without much effort.

Here is the Basic Video Equipment You Need

- 4K Webcam or Your Cellphone
- Tripod
- Desk Ring Light or Standing Ring Light

3. Focus on Audio Quality

Audio is just as important as video quality. Viewers will stop watching if they can't hear you clearly. Consider purchasing an inexpensive lavalier microphone, which can be easily clipped to your clothing and improve the sound of your video.

Choose One of These Audio Equipment Options to Get Started

- Wireless Mic System with a Lavalier and an Adapter for iPhones and Android Phones
- Wired Lavalier Mic with an Adapter for iPhones and Android Phones
- USB Desk Mic with an Adapter for iPhones and Android Phones

4. Set Up a Simple Background

Your background doesn't need to be fancy. A well-lit office or a clean room will work just fine. Make sure the camera is positioned correctly to avoid awkward angles or distractions in the frame.

These Backdrop Options Are Ideal

- Backdrop Stand
- Gray Paper Backdrop

Following these basic steps will allow you to create engaging, professional-looking videos that your audience will enjoy.

Building a YouTube Brand Channel

When setting up your YouTube account, make sure to create a Brand Channel rather than a personal account. A Brand Channel offers several advantages, including the ability to delegate access to team members without sharing your personal login information.

With a Brand Channel, you can manage multiple aspects of your YouTube strategy, such as uploading videos, analyzing performance, and interacting with viewers. It's the best way to organize your business's video marketing efforts on YouTube.

Crafting Effective Calls to Action (CTAs)

Every video you create should have a clear Call to Action (CTA) to guide your audience on what to do next. Whether it's subscribing to your channel, visiting your website, or signing up for your mailing list, an effective CTA will drive action. Additionally, consider using affiliate links to promote products or services relevant to your business. These links can generate additional revenue while providing value to your viewers.

For example, if you're discussing a piece of equipment in your video, include an affiliate link in the description that directs viewers to purchase the product. This type of CTA not only benefits your business but also builds trust with your audience, as you're providing them with useful recommendations.

Maintaining Consistency in Video Marketing

One of the biggest challenges in video for business marketing is maintaining consistency. It's easy to get caught up in perfecting every video, but it's more important to stay on schedule and regularly produce content. Viewers will return to your channel if they know when to expect new videos.

To stay consistent:

- Create a content calendar to plan your videos in advance.
- Set realistic goals for how often you can post videos.
- Focus on delivering value with each video, rather than striving for perfection.

Consistency is key to building a loyal audience and maximizing the impact of your video marketing efforts.

Conclusion

Video for business marketing is essential for small businesses that want to build brand awareness, engage with their audience, and drive conversions. By focusing on high-quality production, tracking key performance indicators, and maintaining consistency, you can create a successful video marketing strategy that elevates your business. Start building your video marketing presence today by setting up your YouTube Brand Channel and producing valuable, engaging content.

Remote Videos

With the digital age in full swing, businesses and creators are shifting to remote setups for high-quality video production. Remote video production allows content creators, business professionals, and filmmakers to create and collaborate on video content without being in the same location. This method leverages high-quality equipment and reliable software to produce seamless videos, sometimes even rivaling traditional, in-studio setups. If you're looking to understand the essentials of remote video production, this guide covers everything you need to know, from equipment to software and tips for achieving professional quality.

What is Remote Video Production?

Remote video production refers to the process of creating video content from multiple, separate locations. Instead of gathering in a single studio, team members operate from different places, recording their parts individually or using real-time video collaboration software. With high-resolution cameras, optimized lighting, and quality audio tools, remote video production has become accessible and straightforward.

This approach allows companies to create consistent content without needing everyone in the same place. By connecting online, production teams can film interviews, presentations, marketing videos, or corporate announcements. Remote video production is an efficient solution that empowers teams to focus on quality, adaptability, and convenience.

Can Video Be Filmed Remotely?

Yes, video can be filmed remotely. In fact, this is becoming the norm in many fields, from corporate training videos to live webinars and brand videos. Whether you're looking to film interviews, tutorials, or live events, remote video production opens up many possibilities.

To film remotely, creators typically use a few essential pieces of equipment: a high-quality camera, lighting tools (usually a ring light), and a microphone. Many modern devices, such as smartphones and webcams, offer high-definition capture capabilities, making it possible to produce clear, sharp footage. Alongside these devices, using a reliable Internet connection and specialized video software ensures smooth communication and video capture.

Platforms like Riverside.fm offer recording capabilities up to 4K resolution, making it an excellent choice for those aiming for superior quality. Such software allows each participant to record their video and audio locally, avoiding the loss of quality due to web-based compression. This setup preserves the highest possible quality and ensures a polished final product, even when filmed remotely.

What are the Benefits of Remote Video Production?

Remote video production provides several advantages that make it a compelling choice for businesses and creators:

- **Flexibility:** Remote production allows teams to work independently from different locations. This setup is particularly useful for businesses with international teams or freelancers.
- **Cost-Efficiency:** By reducing the need for physical studios, travel, and on-location filming, remote production significantly lowers production costs. Teams can save on expenses while maintaining high quality.
- **Adaptability for Business Needs:** Remote video for business helps companies produce consistent content without disrupting daily operations. For businesses aiming to produce regular updates or training videos, this flexibility is invaluable.
- **Enhanced Collaboration:** With remote video production tools, team members can record their parts individually, allowing each person to perfect their contribution without time constraints. They can then collaborate through video calls or real-time feedback platforms.
- **High-Quality Results:** The best remote video recording software, like Riverside.fm, allows creators to record in 4K, ensuring that video and audio quality remain intact. This contrasts with some platforms that compress quality due to Internet limitations.

What is the Difference Between Remote and Local Video Production?

The main difference between remote and local video production lies in the setup and collaboration methods. Local video production occurs on-site, where the team gathers in a studio or specific location. This offers immediate control over lighting, sound, and other visual elements but can limit flexibility due to logistics and location constraints.

On the other hand, remote video production allows each team member to work independently from any location, using specific hardware and software to maintain quality. While local production offers in-person collaboration, remote production allows greater flexibility and access to a wider range of talent, as contributors can participate from anywhere.

Additionally, remote video production can be set up with remote video hardware and tools that make it easy to record, edit, and share footage without losing quality. With Internet-based collaboration, remote production provides a streamlined, adaptable process that suits modern business and creative needs.

Essential Equipment for Filming Video Remotely

Three primary elements are essential for filming remotely: camera, lighting, and sound. Each element plays a critical role in achieving professional results:

- **Camera:** The first thing to consider is camera quality. For a sharp, professional look, use a camera that records at least 1080p resolution. High-quality webcams are a great choice, and many modern smartphones also have advanced cameras that capture in high definition. Just make sure to connect them properly to your recording setup, as standalone smartphone filming can limit connectivity.
- **Lighting:** Lighting is crucial for clarity. Ring lights are popular, as they provide even lighting across the subject's face, enhancing visibility and reducing harsh shadows. If you are filming at a desk, opt for desk-mounted ring lights or lights that attach to your monitor. Consistent lighting creates a professional look that makes a strong impression.
- **Sound:** Sound quality makes a major difference in remote video production. Using a podcast-style USB microphone provides clear, high-quality audio, ensuring that your voice comes across without background noise or distortion. If collaborating with others, use headphones or earbuds to prevent echo and interference.

Remote Video Recording Software

Choosing the best remote video recording software is essential for achieving quality results. While casual meetings can be conducted on Zoom or Microsoft Teams, professional remote production requires higher-resolution software. Here are some recommended options:

- **Riverside.fm:** Known for its ability to record up to 4K video, Riverside.fm is ideal for professional-grade video production. It captures each participant's video and audio locally, ensuring that Internet limitations don't impact quality. Riverside.fm also allows multiple participants, making it suitable for interviews and panel discussions.
- **Zoom:** While not specialized for high-quality video capture, Zoom is a popular choice for business meetings and quick recordings. It compresses video quality, but when paired with good equipment, it can be sufficient for basic needs.
- **OBS Studio:** OBS is a free, open-source platform often used for screen recording and live streaming. While it may require more setup, it provides powerful options for those looking to customize their video production.

Using the right software allows you to maintain high standards and create content that resonates with viewers. With the best remote video recording software, such as Riverside.fm, you can maintain full HD or even 4K resolution, enabling your audience to experience the content as intended.

Tips for Successful Remote Video Production

Finally, a few tips can help ensure that your remote video production is successful:

- **Optimize your background:** A clean, branded background adds professionalism. Avoid clutter and make sure your environment aligns with your brand's guidelines.
- **Invest in a stable Internet connection:** A high-quality video requires a reliable Internet connection. Whenever possible, connect your device directly to the router.
- **Plan your script:** Even if you don't use a strict script, having an outline keeps your message focused and avoids rambling.
- **Engage with the camera:** To maintain viewer interest, consider using hand gestures, maintaining eye contact, and smiling to convey enthusiasm.

Conclusion

Remote video production offers an adaptable and efficient way to create high-quality content. By using the right tools, software, and techniques, creators can overcome the challenges of physical distance and deliver professional, polished videos. For businesses and individuals alike, this approach is valuable in a world where flexibility and high standards are more important than ever. Whether you're producing corporate videos or tutorials, remote video production has the potential to transform your workflow and elevate your output.

Social Media

For small businesses, establishing a social media presence can feel challenging yet vital. Platforms like Facebook, Instagram, Twitter/X, and LinkedIn provide affordable avenues to engage directly with customers, building brand loyalty, increasing visibility, and driving sales. This guide explores how small businesses can maximize the power of social media without overspending. We'll cover initial setup, affordable tools, budgeting tips, and strategies for building a lasting online presence.

Why Do Small Businesses Need Social Media?

Social media is a cost-effective way for small businesses to grow their brand and reach a wider audience. With billions of active users across platforms, businesses can connect with potential customers, showcase their products or services, and build lasting relationships.

Social media offers unique advantages, including:

- **Improved Visibility:** Social media puts your business in front of customers who may not have found you otherwise. Engaging content helps attract new followers and keeps current ones interested.
- **Direct Engagement:** Businesses gain the ability to interact with customers in real-time, responding to comments, questions, or feedback instantly. This direct communication builds trust and demonstrates a commitment to customer service.
- **Data-Driven Insights:** Platforms like Facebook and Instagram provide analytics, helping you understand what types of content perform well. Tracking metrics allows you to adjust strategies for better engagement and conversions.

With social media, even the smallest businesses can level the playing field and establish a brand that resonates with their target audience.

Getting Started: How to Set Up Effective Social Media Profiles

Creating an effective social media profile is more than just setting up an account. Small business owners should focus on crafting profiles that not only look professional but also help drive business objectives. Follow these key steps to get started:

- **Define Key Performance Indicators (KPIs):** KPIs help measure success. For small businesses, essential KPIs include impressions and click-through rates (CTR). Impressions measure how often your content appears in feeds, while CTR tracks how many users click through to your website or landing page. By focusing on these metrics, businesses can gauge how engaging their content is.
- **Optimize Profile Images and Descriptions:** Each platform has specific image dimensions. Ensure your profile and cover images meet these requirements for a polished, professional look. Include a concise yet engaging business description that highlights what sets your brand apart.
- **Utilize Calls to Action (CTA):** Effective social media posts include a strong CTA, guiding viewers to take the next step, such as visiting your website, signing up for a newsletter, or contacting you directly. Clear CTAs drive engagement and conversions.
- **Complete Profile Information:** Platforms allow you to add basic information like business hours, location, and contact details. Take time to fill out every section, as complete profiles are more trustworthy and accessible to customers.

Setting up profiles correctly from the start builds a solid foundation. Professional, well-crafted profiles help your business make a strong first impression.

Social Media Marketing Ideas for Small Businesses

Creating engaging content doesn't have to break the bank. Here are affordable social media marketing ideas for small businesses that boost engagement and strengthen your online presence:

- **Share User-Generated Content:** Showcase content created by your customers. User-generated content is authentic, free, and helps build trust. For instance, encourage customers to share photos of your product and tag your business.
- **Post Behind-the-Scenes Content:** Give followers a glimpse into your daily operations, whether it's a new product being prepared or a team meeting. Behind-the-scenes posts humanize your brand and build a personal connection with your audience.
- **Run Contests and Giveaways:** Boost engagement by running simple contests. Encourage followers to like, share, and tag others for a chance to win. This approach is effective for increasing visibility and reaching new customers.
- **Share Educational Content:** Position yourself as an authority in your industry by posting tips, guides, or "how-to" content. Small businesses that educate their audience gain trust and establish credibility.

Consistency is crucial when posting content. A consistent posting schedule keeps your brand top-of-mind and boosts engagement. Use tools like Hootsuite and Later to schedule content in advance, ensuring your posts reach audiences regularly.

How Much Do Small Businesses Spend on Social Media Marketing?

The cost of social media marketing depends on the business's goals, platform choices, and level of engagement. Here are some general budget guidelines for small businesses:

- **Free Tools:** Many free tools exist to help small businesses manage social media. Hootsuite's free plan allows for three social profiles, making it ideal for businesses getting started on a budget.
- **DIY Content Creation:** Platforms like Canva allow business owners to create high-quality graphics at little to no cost. With Canva's templates, anyone can design professional-looking posts without the need for a graphic designer.
- **Hiring a Small Business Social Media Marketing Agency:** If your business needs more advanced support, consider working with an agency. Small business social media marketing agencies offer a range of services from content creation to analytics.

Budgeting for social media doesn't require significant spending; many small businesses find that consistent, quality content is highly effective.

The Importance of Consistency in Social Media Marketing

Social media algorithms favor accounts that post consistently, which means businesses need to maintain a regular posting schedule. Consistent content keeps audiences engaged and helps your posts appear more frequently in their feeds. Aim to post at least once per week, but for higher engagement, try three to five posts weekly.

To streamline posting, use scheduling tools like Hootsuite or Later. These tools allow you to create and plan content in advance, ensuring a steady flow of posts. Consistency also helps create a sense of predictability, so followers know when to expect updates. Regular engagement builds a loyal audience and strengthens brand awareness.

Working with a Marketing Agency

As your social media presence grows, working with a small business social media marketing agency may be worth considering. An agency brings expertise and resources that can take your strategy to the next level, managing everything from content creation to audience engagement and analytics. Agencies typically offer tiered packages, allowing small businesses to choose the services that fit their budget and goals.

If you're just starting, managing social media independently may be manageable. However, as your business scales, outsourcing can save time and provide professional insights. An agency helps ensure a consistent, high-quality presence across multiple platforms, freeing up time for other areas of your business.

Building a List of Engaged Followers

One of the most important assets a small business can build is a list of engaged followers. Social media platforms occasionally change algorithms, which can impact how often your content reaches followers. By directing followers to your website and encouraging them to sign up for a newsletter, you gain direct access to your audience, bypassing platform limitations.

To grow your email list, make your social media posts actionable. Encourage followers to visit your site and sign up for exclusive offers or updates. Once you have their email, you can maintain communication regardless of social media changes. Email marketing also allows for targeted messaging and personalization, helping you engage followers more effectively.

Conclusion

Affordable social media marketing for small businesses is possible with the right strategies and tools. By focusing on well-optimized profiles, engaging content, and a consistent posting schedule, small businesses can harness the full potential of social media. Remember, a small investment in social media marketing can yield significant returns by enhancing visibility, growing an engaged audience, and driving conversions. Begin implementing these strategies today and watch your brand's social presence flourish.

Podcasts

As digital content expands, podcasts have become a dynamic way for businesses to reach audiences. Podcasts offer flexibility, allowing listeners to tune in while commuting, exercising, or working. A podcast for your business provides a platform to share insights, engage in meaningful conversations, and position your brand as a thought leader.

Starting a podcast might seem challenging, especially for small business owners with limited time. But with the right tools and strategies, launching a podcast can be manageable and affordable. This section will cover everything from initial costs and platform setup to growth strategies, helping you establish a podcast that complements your business goals.

How Much Does It Cost to Create a Podcast?

Costs can vary based on the quality and professionalism you aim to achieve. Below is a breakdown of typical expenses:

- **Microphone:** For clear audio, consider a quality microphone. Entry-level models like the Audio-Technica ATR2100x USB are available for around $80. Professional-grade mics, such as the Shure SM7B, cost between $400 and $500, offering top-notch sound.
- **Headphones:** Noise-isolating headphones improve audio editing and recording quality. High-quality options, like Audio-Technica or Sennheiser models, start around $100.
- **Recording Software:** Many podcasters use free software like Audacity. Alternatively, Adobe Audition is popular among professionals and costs around $20 per month.
- **Hosting Platform:** While free platforms like Spotify for Podcasters (formerly Anchor.fm) exist, paid hosting providers like Podbean and Buzzsprout cost between $5 and $20 per month, offering better analytics and distribution options.

Estimated total cost: If you opt for basic equipment, you can launch a podcast for under $200. A professional setup might reach $500 or more, but quality equipment pays off by providing a polished, engaging listening experience.

I'll outline a few tricks for saving money (and time) below.

Do You Need a License to Start a Podcast?

No specific license is required to launch a podcast. However, certain considerations are necessary:

- **Music Licensing:** If you use music, it must be royalty-free or licensed. You can find royalty-free tracks from websites like PremiumBeat or Epidemic Sound. Avoid using popular music unless you purchase proper licensing to avoid copyright issues.
- **Copyrighted Material:** Ensure all content, such as quotes, audio clips, or guest contributions, are free from copyright issues. Original content is always the safest route for podcasts.

With these precautions, you can avoid potential legal issues and focus on creating original, valuable content that reflects your brand's expertise.

Do You Get Paid if You Start a Podcast?

Monetizing a podcast is possible, though it typically requires a consistent audience. Common ways to earn revenue from podcasting include:

- **Sponsorships:** Sponsors pay to feature their product or service on your podcast. As your audience grows, sponsorship opportunities increase. Most sponsors look for niche podcasts with dedicated listeners.
- **Listener Donations:** Platforms like Patreon allow loyal fans to support you financially. Creating bonus content or offering shout-outs can incentivize support.
- **Advertising Networks:** Spotify for Podcasters, for instance, connects podcasters with advertisers, allowing you to earn through ad placements. Although smaller podcasts may not qualify initially, growing your audience can attract advertisers.

Monetizing a podcast takes time, but with consistency and strategic partnerships, you can eventually generate income from your episodes.

How to Start a Podcast with No Audience

Launching without an existing audience is challenging but achievable. Here's a step-by-step guide:

- **Define Your Niche:** Identify the topics most relevant to your industry and potential audience. Focusing on a specific niche helps you stand out from other podcasts and attracts listeners interested in your expertise.
- **Develop High-Quality Content:** Plan episodes that provide practical advice, insightful interviews, or case studies. High-value content keeps listeners engaged and encourages word-of-mouth growth.
- **Leverage Social Media:** Promote episodes on platforms like LinkedIn, Facebook, and Instagram. Share short clips or quotes to attract potential listeners, gradually growing your audience.
- **Engage with Your Guests' Networks:** Interviewing industry experts is an excellent way to reach new listeners. When guests share the episode with their followers, your podcast gains credibility and visibility.

With consistent, valuable content and a proactive approach to promotion, you can steadily build a loyal audience.

How to Automate Episode Creation with Existing Content

For business owners short on time, automating podcast episodes is an efficient solution:

- **Use Existing Videos:** Repurpose video content created by following the recommendations I made earlier in the book. Upload the video to a platform like Spotify for Podcasters to convert it into a podcast episode effortlessly.
- **Read Existing Blog Content:** Take blog posts created using the blog guidelines outlined in this book, record yourself reading them aloud, and upload the audio as a new episode. This approach creates valuable, time-saving content for your audience.

Automating episodes with existing content not only saves time and money but also provides diverse, consistent material for listeners, enhancing your podcast's appeal.

Setting Up a Spotify for Podcasters Account

Spotify for Podcasters is a straightforward, free platform for hosting your podcast. Here's how to set up your account:

1. **Sign Up:** Go to Spotify for Podcasters and create an account. Use a dedicated email address for easy account management.
2. **Upload Episodes:** Upload an audio file, input your podcast's name and description, and choose relevant categories to make your podcast easily searchable.
3. **Set Up Your Branding:** Customize the cover art, description, and episode titles to reflect your brand's tone. Spotify for Podcasters also allows you to manage multiple episodes, set release dates, and organize episodes by season.

Spotify for Podcasters is an ideal platform for small business podcasters due to its accessibility and wide reach.

Distributing Your Podcast to Major Platforms

To maximize your reach, submit your podcast to multiple directories:

- **Spotify's RSS Feed:** Spotify for Podcasters automatically generates an RSS feed for your podcast. Copy this feed link for distribution.
- **Apple Podcasts:** Visit Apple Podcasts Connect, sign up, and paste your RSS feed. Once approved, your podcast will be listed on Apple Podcasts.
- **Amazon Music:** Go to the Amazon Music portal, sign up, and submit your RSS feed. This allows Amazon Music users to find and listen to your episodes.

Expanding to major directories maximizes discoverability and attracts a wider audience across devices and platforms.

Expanding Your Reach Across Podcast Platforms

After listing on Spotify, Apple Podcasts, and Amazon Music, consider expanding to additional platforms:

- **Castbox:** Known for easy access and user engagement, Castbox attracts podcast listeners globally.
- **Goodpods:** This platform focuses on community interaction, helping listeners discover shows through recommendations.
- **iHeartRadio:** With a large user base, iHeartRadio offers valuable exposure, especially in the U.S. market.
- **Overcast:** Popular among iOS users, Overcast is known for advanced listening features.
- **Pocket Casts:** This platform's customizability and strong recommendation engine can attract loyal listeners.
- **Radio Public:** As an independent platform, Radio Public supports smaller podcasts, making it ideal for niche shows.

Distributing across multiple platforms enhances accessibility, helping you grow your audience and solidify your presence in the podcasting community.

Final Thoughts

Starting a podcast for your small business requires planning, time, and a commitment to quality. However, the benefits are substantial: a well-executed podcast can attract new customers, strengthen your brand, and establish you as a trusted voice in your industry. By following this guide - selecting the right equipment, utilizing existing content, and maximizing distribution - you can create a podcast that captivates listeners and elevates your business.

Nurturing Emails

Nurturing emails are essential tools for building and maintaining customer relationships, typically taking the form of email newsletters or email drip campaigns. While both approaches aim to engage audiences over time, they serve slightly different purposes.

Email newsletters are generally sent on a regular schedule (weekly, monthly, etc.) and provide updates, valuable insights, and company news, keeping your brand top of mind.

On the other hand, email drip campaigns are automated, time-based sequences that deliver targeted content based on specific user actions or time intervals. Drip campaigns guide recipients through a planned journey - introducing them to your brand, addressing their needs, and gradually moving them toward a purchase decision.

Together, newsletters and drip campaigns offer a balanced approach to nurturing, with newsletters fostering ongoing engagement and drip campaigns driving conversion-focused interactions.

Newsletters

A newsletter remains one of the most powerful and cost-effective marketing tools for small businesses. In an age dominated by social media and search engine algorithms, owning your audience through a newsletter gives you control over communication and engagement. A well-crafted newsletter can drive traffic back to your website, build relationships, and ultimately grow your business. This section will explore what a newsletter should include, how to set it up, and why it's an essential part of your digital marketing strategy. We'll also address common questions such as why some newsletters fail and whether they are still profitable today.

What Is a Newsletter in Business?

A newsletter is a digital marketing tool used to regularly communicate with customers, leads, or a targeted audience through email. Typically, it contains a mix of company updates, industry news, and valuable content designed to educate, engage, or inspire action. The primary purpose of a newsletter is to keep your audience informed about your brand while offering something of value. Unlike transactional emails, which serve a specific purpose (e.g., order confirmations or password resets), newsletters build long-term relationships.

The content and tone of a newsletter can vary depending on the audience and goals. For example, a B2B company may focus on thought leadership, sharing white papers or case studies, while a retail company might feature new products or promotions. A well-crafted business letter email format balances promotional material with helpful information, ensuring that the newsletter feels valuable rather than overly sales-driven.

In the digital age, where consumers are inundated with content, newsletters give you a direct line to your audience. Unlike social media platforms, where algorithms control who sees your posts, newsletters go straight to the inbox of subscribers who have opted in to hear from you. This means you're reaching an audience that is already interested in your business.

What Should a Newsletter Include?

At its core, a successful newsletter offers value to the reader while subtly advancing your business objectives. The balance between informative content and promotional material is key to maintaining long-term engagement. Below are the essential elements that every newsletter should include:

- **Valuable Content:** Include information that helps your audience solve a problem, learn something new, or stay informed about your industry. For example, if you're in the tech industry, include updates on the latest software or hardware trends. You might also share company news, product updates, or links to recent blog posts. A newsletter example could feature articles with tips for optimizing business operations, short industry news blurbs, or "how-to" guides that address common customer pain points.

- **Consistent Schedule:** Consistency is one of the most important factors in email marketing success. It's recommended to send a newsletter at least once a month but not more than twice a month unless the content is highly valuable. Subscribers appreciate a predictable rhythm, and your business stays top-of-mind without overwhelming inboxes.

- **Personalization:** Personalized emails have higher open and click-through rates. Use your customer data to customize your newsletters. Address recipients by name, tailor content to their preferences, or use segmentation to send different emails to different groups. A personalized newsletter shows that you understand your audience and are sending them information that is relevant to their interests.

- **Calls to Action (CTAs):** Make sure each newsletter has a clear CTA. Whether it's "Download our free guide," "Shop our new collection," or "Watch our latest video," your CTA should guide readers toward taking a specific action. This could be as simple as including a button at the end of an article or linking back to a blog post.

- **Visually Appealing Layout:** The design and layout of your newsletter play a critical role in readability and engagement. Use a clean, visually appealing newsletter template that is responsive on both desktop and mobile devices. A good layout highlights your main message, uses readable fonts, and incorporates attractive images without overwhelming the reader.

- **Engaging Subject Lines:** The subject line is the first thing your subscribers see. An effective subject line grabs attention, encourages curiosity, and hints at the value inside the email. Avoid overly promotional language; instead, try to offer something your readers genuinely care about, like "5 Tips for Growing Your Business This Month" or "Exclusive Access to Our Latest Product Line."

How to Build a Newsletter

Building a newsletter from scratch might seem daunting, but breaking the process down into manageable steps makes it much easier. Here's a comprehensive guide to help you set up a successful newsletter:

1. **Set Up Your Mailing List:** The first step is to make sure you have a functional sign-up form on your website. Whether through a dedicated landing page, a blog pop-up, or an embedded form in your site's footer, you want to make it easy for visitors to subscribe. This form should integrate with your email marketing service, such as Mailchimp or Constant Contact, so that new subscribers are automatically added to your list.
    Tip: Ask for "First Name", and "Last Name" in addition to an email address.
2. **Choose the Right Platform:** Choosing the right platform is crucial for long-term success. Starting with a tool like Mailchimp offers great flexibility for beginners and advanced users alike. With Mailchimp, you can automate your newsletter by connecting your RSS feed, ensuring that new content is sent out regularly. Other platforms like HubSpot, Zoho, and Constant Contact also provide excellent features, so consider your specific needs when selecting one.
3. **Automate the Process:** Automation saves time and ensures consistency. If you have a blog on your website, you can use an RSS feed to automatically pull content into your newsletters. For example, you can schedule the newsletter to send whenever new blog posts are published or on a regular basis, featuring a roundup of recent posts. This reduces manual work and ensures that your content stays fresh and timely.
4. **Design the Newsletter:** An effective design should be clean, visually appealing, and aligned with your brand. Use a customizable newsletter template that reflects your brand's colors and tone. Break the content into sections with clear headings, include relevant images, and make sure there are no large blocks of text. Don't forget to make the email mobile-friendly, as a large portion of your audience will likely read it on their smartphones.
5. **Test and Optimize:** Before hitting "send," always test your newsletter. Check that the layout displays correctly on both desktop and mobile

devices, verify that all links and CTAs work, and ensure that the images load properly. After sending, track open rates, click-through rates, and conversions to see how your audience is engaging with your content. Use this data to make improvements in future campaigns.

6. **Promote Your Newsletter:** Don't assume people will find your newsletter on their own. Promote your sign-up form across all of your marketing channels, including your website, social media profiles, blog posts, and even during webinars or podcasts. Incentivize sign-ups with exclusive content, discounts, or a free resource.

Why Do Most Newsletters Fail?

Many newsletters fail due to a lack of strategy, value, or consistency.

Here are some common reasons:

- **Irrelevant or Poor Content:** If the content doesn't align with your subscribers' interests or fails to offer value, they will stop opening your emails. Ensure your content is engaging, informative, and tailored to the needs of your audience.
- **Inconsistent Scheduling:** Sending emails too frequently can overwhelm your subscribers, while sending too infrequently causes them to forget about your business. A regular, predictable schedule fosters trust and keeps your brand top-of-mind.
- **Lack of Personalization:** Generic newsletters don't resonate with subscribers. Personalizing your emails with the subscriber's name or segmented content will make your emails more relevant and engaging.
- **Poor Design and Functionality:** A poorly designed newsletter can discourage engagement. Ensure your design is clean and that all links and images function properly. Test your emails to make sure they display correctly on different devices and email platforms.

To avoid these pitfalls, focus on delivering consistent value, knowing your audience, and keeping your email content and frequency manageable.

What Is the Best Program to Create a Newsletter?

The best program for creating a newsletter depends on your business needs and technical expertise. Below are some popular options:

- **Mailchimp:** Mailchimp is a popular choice for small businesses due to its easy-to-use interface and flexible automation features. One of its best features is the ability to connect your RSS feed to automatically send newsletters whenever you publish new content. Additionally, Mailchimp offers customizable templates, advanced reporting, and integration with numerous tools.
- **Constant Contact:** Known for its excellent customer support, Constant Contact is a solid option for businesses looking for a user-friendly platform with pre-designed templates. It's a great tool for managing contacts, running drip campaigns, and sending engaging emails.
- **HubSpot:** HubSpot provides robust marketing automation features and is ideal for businesses looking to integrate their email marketing with CRM and lead generation tools. The platform is highly customizable and scalable for growing businesses.

Are Newsletters Still Profitable?

Absolutely! Newsletters remain one of the most profitable marketing channels when executed correctly. The profitability of newsletters lies in their ability to build and maintain a direct line of communication with your audience. Here are several reasons why newsletters continue to be a great investment:

- **High Return on Investment (ROI):** Email marketing consistently delivers one of the highest ROIs of any digital marketing channel. A well-targeted and engaged email list can generate significant revenue through product sales, service promotions, and repeat business.
- **Low Cost:** Compared to paid advertising (such as Google and Facebook/Instagram ads), newsletters are relatively inexpensive to create and distribute. Once you've built a list of subscribers, there are minimal ongoing costs associated with sending out regular emails.
- **Direct Audience Connection:** Unlike social media, where algorithms dictate who sees your content, newsletters allow you to communicate directly with your audience. This control over your communication is invaluable, especially during product launches or major announcements.
- **Customer Retention:** Regular newsletters help maintain relationships with customers, keeping them engaged with your brand over time. Engaged customers are more likely to make repeat purchases, refer friends, and provide valuable feedback.

Conclusion

Building a business newsletter doesn't have to be complicated, but it does require a strategic approach. By following the key steps outlined here - setting up your mailing list, choosing the right platform, automating processes, and sending valuable content - you can create a newsletter that drives engagement, strengthens customer relationships, and boosts profitability. Remember, consistency is key, and your calls to action must work flawlessly. When done right, your newsletter can become one of the most valuable assets in your digital marketing toolbox.

Email Drip Campaigns

An email drip campaign is a pre-scheduled series of emails sent to prospects or customers over time. Each email in the series is carefully timed to help guide recipients toward a specific action, such as signing up for a service, making a purchase, or engaging further with a brand. Unlike traditional email marketing, where emails are sent in bulk, drip campaigns deliver personalized content gradually, often triggered by user actions or time intervals.

These campaigns are particularly effective for small businesses, allowing you to connect with potential customers without having to manually manage each communication. Drip campaigns help build relationships by delivering consistent value, whether through education, updates, or incentives. When automated using reliable email drip campaign software, these campaigns ensure that each contact receives the right message at the right time, helping small businesses maintain engagement and nurture leads effortlessly.

Why Small Businesses Should Use Email Drip Campaigns

Email drip campaigns allow small businesses to scale their marketing efforts without a huge time investment. They can be tailored to align with other efforts, enabling businesses to follow up on leads generated through other channels. By nurturing prospects with email, small businesses can maximize conversion rates by keeping potential customers engaged and informed until they are ready to buy.

Building an Effective Email Drip Campaign for Small Businesses

For small businesses, a structured approach to email drip campaigns can make all the difference. Here's a sequence tailored specifically to help small businesses nurture leads and convert them into customers:

1. **Welcome Aboard:** Start with a welcome email that introduces your business and sets expectations.
2. **Solving the Problem:** Identify and address a common problem your target audience faces, positioning your product or service as the solution.
3. **Customer Proof:** Use testimonials or case studies to build credibility and trust.
4. **Real Talk:** Acknowledge potential objections and ease any concerns that prospects may have.
5. **Closing the Sale:** End with a compelling call to action that encourages prospects to make a purchase.

Here's an in-depth guide to each of these emails:

1. Welcome Aboard

The first email in a drip campaign should greet new subscribers warmly and introduce your business. This email can also provide a roadmap for what subscribers can expect from future emails, helping to build anticipation. For small businesses, the welcome email is an opportunity to make a positive first impression. Personalize this message by addressing the recipient by name, and consider offering something of value, such as a discount code or access to exclusive content.

For example, if your business provides fitness coaching, the welcome email could include a "welcome gift" like a free one-week workout plan. This helps recipients feel immediately engaged and provides an early incentive to explore your offerings further.

2. Solving the Problem

In the second email, focus on a specific problem your target audience faces and introduce your product or service as the solution. This email should demonstrate your understanding of the recipient's needs and build a connection by showing empathy. By addressing a pain point, you position your product as essential rather than optional.

For example, if you're a financial advisor, this email might discuss common challenges small business owners face when managing cash flow. Then, you could explain how your advisory services help alleviate these issues, giving the reader a reason to keep considering your services. Including examples that highlight similar solutions can also strengthen your message by showing how your approach has worked in real scenarios.

3. Customer Proof

Testimonials play a critical role in any sales process. In this email, include stories from past customers who benefited from your product or service. Real-life examples, especially those that quantify results, can make your offering feel more tangible. Highlighting relatable successes helps build trust and makes prospective clients more comfortable considering your solution.

For instance, if you own a digital marketing agency, you could share a testimonial from a client whose business achieved a significant increase in sales after using your services. Adding a direct quote from the customer, along with a compelling statistic, makes the story more believable and engaging.

4. Real Talk

In the fourth email, acknowledge potential hesitations that may keep a lead from converting. Perhaps the price seems high, or there's uncertainty about the product's fit. Address these objections directly to put potential customers at ease. If pricing is a common concern, for example, explain how the investment pays off in the long run or offer a breakdown of the product's value.

Imagine your business is a software-as-a-service (SaaS) company targeting small businesses. A common objection might be that small business owners are hesitant to invest in new technology. In this email, you could outline the simplicity of your software, how quickly they can see results, or share a free demo link. Transparency fosters trust, and it's often the difference between a lead choosing your brand or a competitor's.

5. Closing the Sale

The final email in the drip sequence should drive recipients toward a decision. This email is about reframing your product or service as a smart investment and the logical next step. Shift the reader's perspective from "why buy now?" to "why wait?" Your language should create a sense of urgency without feeling pushy.

For example, you might offer a limited-time discount or a special bonus to those who sign up by a certain date. This helps nudge hesitant leads toward taking action. Additionally, reinforce your call to action by summarizing the benefits and impact of your product or service.

Frequently Asked Questions About Email Drip Campaigns

How Many Emails Should Be in a Drip Campaign?

Most small businesses find that a series of 4-6 emails works best. This range allows enough touchpoints to nurture the lead without overwhelming the recipient. Start with 4-6 emails, then experiment by adding or removing messages based on your audience's response. Use email drip campaign software like Mailchimp to monitor engagement metrics like open and click-through rates to optimize your sequence over time.

Do Drip Campaigns Really Work?

Absolutely. Studies consistently show that drip campaigns are highly effective, leading to higher open and engagement rates compared to one-off emails. When done right, drip campaigns nurture leads over time, build trust, and increase conversions. For small businesses, email drip campaigns are one of the most affordable and scalable ways to reach new customers. When combined with other marketing channels you can boost the campaign's effectiveness by drawing in new leads and keeping them engaged.

How Long Should a Drip Campaign Last?

The length of a drip campaign depends on your business model and sales cycle. Generally, drip campaigns span one to three weeks, ensuring consistent engagement without overwhelming the recipient. For longer sales cycles, such as those involving high-ticket items, you may want a campaign that stretches to six weeks or more, with a greater interval between emails. Testing and analyzing the performance with email drip campaign software will help you determine the ideal duration for your audience.

Email Drip Campaign Best Practices

Creating an effective email drip campaign requires a blend of strategy, timing, and personalization. Here are some best practices to keep in mind:

- **Segment your audience:** Not all leads are the same. Segment your audience based on demographics, behavior, or purchasing history to ensure they receive relevant messages.
- **Focus on value:** Make sure each email provides value, whether it's an educational tip, a special offer, or insightful industry data. This keeps recipients engaged and positions your brand as a trusted resource.
- **Keep it concise:** While it's tempting to include all the details in every email, concise and engaging messages tend to perform better.
- **Optimize for mobile:** With the majority of emails being read on mobile devices, ensure your content is responsive and easy to read on smaller screens.
- **Use strong CTAs:** Every email should have a clear call to action that tells the recipient exactly what to do next, whether it's downloading a resource, booking a consultation, or making a purchase.

Conclusion

A well-planned email drip campaign is an invaluable asset for small businesses looking to build meaningful connections with their audience. By delivering targeted messages at each stage of the customer journey, you can guide prospects from initial interest to final purchase with ease and efficiency. Remember to focus on providing value, addressing customer pain points, and using testimonials to build trust. With the right structure, consistent messaging, and effective use of email drip campaign software, your business can nurture leads, increase engagement, and drive conversions. A strategic email drip campaign is more than a marketing tool - it's a long-term investment in customer relationships and business growth.

Interpreting Your Results

Results are where the marketing industry gets a little shady. Small business owners are painfully familiar with fly-by-night marketers who knock on their door and promise the moon.

The truth is that some of your results will be direct and some will be more indirect. You'll get sales but you'll also get window shoppers. It's all good - as long as you know how to turn those window shoppers into buyers.

This is what success looks like when you repurpose content.

Paid Media Results

These are far and away the easiest to analyze. As long as you have your reporting tools configured correctly you'll be able to see if the leads you're getting are worth more than you're paying for the ads.

Give each paid media campaign 3 - 6 months and if you're not seeing a return on your investment by then it's time to try something else.

SEO Results

Search engine optimization (SEO) relates to your organic (unpaid) listings in Google. Users who find you through those results are unlikely to be clients. They're more likely to be people that are browsing or looking for information. Window shoppers.

But that's okay!

Think of it as speed dating. Maybe one of those speed dates will work out, but we're mostly creating an opportunity to get information where that opportunity never existed before.

During speed dating, you provide basic information about yourself. How you look at the world, for example, or what your story is. You're not proposing marriage or a cross-country road trip. You're just trying to get a second date if things seem right in your brief moments together.

On a website, your speed date is your transitional call to action. And your "second date" is the user's legitimate email address. If you have their email, you have opportunities to stay in front of them. In marketing we refer to this as a nurturing campaign.

Aside from a sale, a customer's email address is the most valuable thing you can capture for marketing purposes. So you have the customer's information. You've never had that before.

Now, you can *finally* go spearfishing.

SEO is unlikely to be a direct source for clients. But over time, especially as you continue to improve the quality of your blog posts and your videos, the quality of your website traffic will improve, and you'll start collecting those email addresses.

For a brand new website, the typical conversion percentage rate will be between 0.5% and 1%. Our goal is to reach a minimum of 3% as quickly as possible. And it happens! I've seen conversion rates as high as 20%, which is pretty uncommon. Really good campaigns, however, usually convert between 5% and 10%.

So your SEO results might not be earth-shattering, especially at first. But you're creating and empowering your marketing machine.

By creating blog posts, getting people to your website, and giving them a reason to share their email addresses, you'll have the ability to reach them again. You can, for example, send them new blog posts through your newsletter. You're creating opportunities to follow up and go spearfishing. And those are the results we're really looking for from SEO.

Social Media Results

The next place where you'll get results is social media. These are the primary social media channels to use:

- Twitter/X
- Instagram and TikTok
- LinkedIn
- Facebook

Twitter/X

Real talk alert: it's pretty unlikely to see results from Twitter/X, especially right away. Developing an audience on Twitter/X takes a long time. Also, Twitter/X users are usually looking for short snippets, which isn't ideal for marketing.

Google references Twitter/X, however, and Twitter/X activity is an indicator of a website's legitimacy, so use Twitter/X for those reasons. Direct ROI from Twitter/X traffic is rare, but your likelihood of getting results varies depending on whether you offer B2B or B2C services.

Instagram and TikTok

If you're a B2C company that offers products or services to consumers, you might see some results from social media like Instagram or TikTok.

The challenge is that social media platforms aren't particularly friendly to organic traffic for businesses. It's a well-known fact that these platforms' algorithms bury organic business-related content. They prefer to get businesses to pay for traffic.

That said, social media is still an extremely powerful way to communicate with your user base. And there is value in the credibility that producing consistent content provides.

Also, your results from Instagram and TikTok will probably be the lowest of the remaining three platforms, as Instagram and TikTok do not give you an easy way to provide calls to action in organic posts.

For example, unless you pay for an ad, users have to click a link in your Instagram bio to leave the app. And that's not something people do all that often on social media. Instagram knows this and they're counting on you to buy ads from them to get around the limitation. But we're more clever than that.

Instagram is less about driving conversions and more about staying in front of your user base. If people choose to follow you, however, Instagram's algorithm *should* show those users your posts. And with more and more people using Instagram and TikTok this just makes that blue ocean bigger.

LinkedIn

You would think LinkedIn would have the highest potential for B2B marketing, right? Sometimes it does, depending on what you're selling, but most users don't open LinkedIn with a "ready-to-buy" mindset.

LinkedIn is more like a business-card-trading online platform. It's not quite as "social" as other social media platforms.

With that said, LinkedIn has a lot of untapped potential. And if it continues to grow, you'll want to be established there. Businesses use it primarily as an organic social advertising tool. Recent advances in AI content authoring have blown this door wide open.

If you have a good presence on LinkedIn, and if that presence requires essentially zero additional effort from you or your team, there are opportunities to drive results. But don't expect to see too much from LinkedIn, or Twitter/X, Instagram, or TikTok.

Facebook

Facebook has more potential for traction in comparison to the above platforms, especially if your posts induce engagement and you pay to boost them. That's where Facebook will shine as a marketing channel.

If your audience is on Facebook, you'll probably see the most effective results there, including conversions and clicks to your website. Remember, clicks to your website are the first step in getting legitimate conversions.

Facebook typically has the highest potential of the social platforms.

Even still, you'll probably see more results from your SEO efforts over time. Next in line will be social media, and then finally, at a distant third, will be your podcast.

Podcast Results

The results you can get from podcasts depend on the value of your offering, and how closely your offer relates to your product.

For example, if your business offers online classes, and you can offer those online classes in your podcast, you'll have a decent chance of converting traffic through that channel. But most companies' offers aren't that closely related.

Most companies offer a service or sell a product, and plugging your product in your podcast gets tricky. If you're going to sell your product through a podcast, it would usually be as an ad or sponsorship on someone else's podcast.

But podcasts give you a platform to speak directly to your audience. It's a low-cost way to get your story across in a format that users find appealing. And if your audience finds you organically through your blogs, you can invite them to listen to your podcast, further expanding your net.

Moreover, instead of being on Google alone, you're also on iTunes and on Spotify. Podcasts increase the number of search engines you appear in because iTunes and Spotify are search engines, too.

All that said, the direct results from your podcast are probably going to be the lowest of the marketing channels.

But there's still value in getting that content out there. And frankly, it feels pretty cool to be able to say, "Hey, I have a podcast."

A podcast adds legitimacy to your brand. It makes people take you more seriously as an authority in your industry.

You're going to see some conversions from podcasts, but probably not many. Never say never, however - especially if you have a compelling call to action built into your podcast.

The Content Marketing Flywheel

The real results come from the flywheel you set in motion when you publish content across all of these channels.

If you have enough content on social media, you can leverage that content to build your social media following.

With that following, you can create a social media environment or ecosystem "around" your business. And if you're investing in that, you'll see more clicks and more results from your website, which makes your website more legitimate in Google's eyes.

And when your website is legitimate in Google's eyes, your organic search engine rankings will improve. As you get those pages ranking in the number one, two, and three positions, you'll see a significant amount of traffic to your website.

And if your website is optimized to convert that traffic, you're going to start to see serious conversions from your organic efforts.

These conversions will come in the form of additions to your mailing list. Your growing mailing list is the result of all of these efforts. Finkle is Einhorn. Einhorn is Finkle.

Executing the Marketing Campaign

For small businesses, marketing isn't just about reaching more customers; it's about building a sustainable, loyal customer base that understands and values what your business offers. This guide will answer key questions around small business marketing strategy to help you make informed decisions, from creating a targeted plan to selecting the best marketing channels. This strategy can elevate your business and guide you to long-term success.

Reporting

A marketing report is a strategic document that compiles key data and insights about your marketing efforts. It's more than just numbers – it's a tool to understand how your campaigns are impacting your business. This document serves as a foundation for strategic adjustments, helping small business owners optimize their marketing strategies and make informed decisions about resource allocation.

In a small business setting, a marketing report highlights essential metrics and KPIs (Key Performance Indicators) that indicate your marketing effectiveness. Tracking metrics like traffic sources, customer behavior, and conversions can provide clarity on what works and what doesn't. A well-constructed report allows business owners to understand customer journeys, identify gaps, and adjust their efforts accordingly to maximize ROI.

While some small businesses overlook marketing reports, establishing a reporting process doesn't have to be complex. With basic tools like Google Analytics and a consistent reporting framework, even small teams can manage effective reporting that supports data-driven decisions.

What is in a Marketing Report?

A comprehensive marketing report generally includes several key sections that capture both high-level and detailed insights. Here's what you should include in an effective marketing report:

- **Overview of Goals and KPIs:** Begin with a brief overview of your main goals, which could be brand awareness, lead generation, or conversions. Include KPIs that align with these goals.
- **Traffic Metrics:** Track data on website visits, traffic sources, and user demographics. Knowing where your audience comes from and how they engage with your site can shape future strategies.
- **Conversion Metrics:** Conversions, such as completed forms or purchases, represent your primary lagging KPI. These metrics show if your efforts lead to actual customer actions.
- **Lead Quality:** Evaluate the quality of leads to ensure your campaigns attract the right audience. Qualifying questions on forms can help assess lead potential, saving time for your sales team.
- **ROI and Cost Analysis:** Include the return on investment (ROI) for each campaign. For example, if you invest in a pay-per-click (PPC) campaign, track how much revenue that effort generates compared to the ad spend.
- **Campaign Highlights and Insights:** Summarize key findings and insights from your campaigns, noting what worked, what didn't, and any adjustments made to improve performance.

What Does a Good Marketing Report Look Like?

A good marketing report is organized, clear, and directly relevant to your goals. It should communicate performance in a way that's accessible to all stakeholders, even if they aren't marketing experts. Each metric should align with your KPIs, and the data should be segmented for clarity.

Here's what to include in a well-structured marketing report:

1. Clear Objectives

Outline your objectives at the top of the report. If your goal is to increase brand awareness, emphasize metrics like website traffic, social media reach, and engagement rates. For lead generation, highlight metrics on conversions and lead quality. Clear objectives help align the report with broader business goals, making the data actionable.

2. Detailed Metrics with Segmentation

Metrics should be broken down by channels, audience demographics, and user behavior. This segmentation allows you to see where your strategy excels and where there's room for improvement. For instance, tracking website traffic by source (e.g., organic, paid, social) shows which channels drive the most engagement.

3. Comparison with Benchmarks

To assess your success, compare current performance with historical data or industry benchmarks. If conversions this month surpass the previous month's, that's an indicator of positive growth. Regularly benchmarking your metrics helps track progress and identify trends over time.

4. Data Visualization

Graphs, charts, and tables make complex data accessible. A simple line graph showing traffic growth over the past six months is easier to interpret than a list of numbers. Visuals make the report more engaging and quickly communicate insights to all readers.

Consider starting with the funnel detailed toward the beginning of this book.

How to Generate a Marketing Report

Creating a marketing report involves identifying your goals, setting up tracking, and using tools to gather and present data. Here's a step-by-step guide to building a marketing report:

Step 1: Define Your KPIs

Before diving into data collection, define your leading and lagging KPIs. Leading KPIs, such as website traffic, provide early signals on campaign performance. Lagging KPIs, such as completed purchases or filled-out forms, indicate final outcomes. These KPIs give structure to your report and help focus on metrics that directly impact your business.

Step 2: Set Up Tracking with Google Analytics

Google Analytics is a powerful, free tool that provides comprehensive tracking capabilities. Work with your webmaster to install Google Analytics on all pages of your site. Configure tracking for critical pages like landing pages and "thank you" pages, and set goals that reflect your KPIs, such as form submissions or sales. Proper setup ensures your data is accurate and meaningful.

Step 3: Use a Marketing Report Template

Using a marketing report template simplifies the reporting process. Templates standardize your data presentation, making it easier to compare metrics over time and communicate findings effectively. Many templates are customizable, allowing you to adjust sections based on the campaigns you're tracking.

Step 4: Compile and Segment Data

Gather data from your marketing channels and segment it by campaign, demographic, or source. For instance, segmenting email and social media performance separately allows you to see which channels yield the best results. Using a marketing reporting tool can streamline data collection from multiple platforms, making reporting more efficient.

Step 5: Analyze and Interpret Data

After gathering your data, analyze it against your KPIs and objectives. Look for patterns, such as high engagement on specific content or a decline in conversion rates on certain days. Your analysis should provide actionable insights that inform future strategies.

How to Use Google Analytics in Marketing Reporting

Google Analytics is essential for tracking KPIs and optimizing your marketing strategy.

To get started:

1. Set Up Goals in Google Analytics

Goals allow you to track specific actions on your site, like filling out a form or completing a purchase. Configure a goal by selecting the "thank you" page URL as the goal destination. Each time a user completes a form and reaches this page, it counts as a goal completion, tracking your website's conversion rate accurately.

The configuration is slightly different for ecommerce sites but the same concepts apply.

2. Use Behavior Flow Analysis

Behavior flow analysis shows how users navigate through your website. It reveals which pages draw the most attention, where users drop off, and which content keeps visitors engaged. This insight helps optimize the customer journey, increasing the likelihood of conversions.

3. Explore Audience Demographics

Demographic data, such as age, location, and interests, helps tailor your marketing efforts to resonate with your target audience. For instance, if a significant portion of your audience comes from a specific location, consider focusing more resources on local campaigns.

4. Leverage Campaign Tracking

Use Google Analytics to track individual campaigns by setting up UTM parameters. These parameters allow you to identify which campaigns drive traffic and conversions, providing detailed insight into campaign performance. This feature is particularly useful for tracking paid ads, email newsletters, and social media promotions.

Planning

Creating a strong small business marketing strategy requires focusing on a few essential elements that ensure alignment with your audience's needs.

Marketing Calendar

Marketing requires consistency, and one of the best ways to achieve this is by implementing a structured marketing calendar. A marketing calendar lays out your entire plan, keeping you organized and ensuring that you're posting and advertising consistently. This helps potential customers remember your brand and builds trust over time.

When setting up your marketing calendar, consider these factors:

- **Plan for seasonality:** For instance, real estate agents may allocate more of their ad budget for the busy summer season, while event planners may adjust for wedding or trade show seasons.
- **Set consistent posting schedules:** This is especially important for social media. Posting randomly can hurt visibility and engagement, so stick to a regular schedule.
- **Batch content creation:** Creating content ahead of time allows you to stick to the calendar even during busy periods, helping maintain consistency and saving time.

Testing and Adjustment

Marketing is an ongoing process of testing, learning, and improving. By monitoring your results regularly, you can make informed adjustments to your strategy. Testing different messages, formats, or offers helps identify what resonates most with your audience, maximizing your return on investment (ROI).

Consider using tools like Hotjar to analyze user behavior on your website, such as where they click, scroll, or hover. Survey tools like SurveyMonkey allow you to reach out for feedback, gaining insights directly from customers that can guide future adjustments.

By consistently testing, adjusting, and refining your approach, you can set your business up for lasting success.

The Review Process

The frequency of reporting depends on the goals and scale of your campaigns. For small businesses, weekly and monthly reporting intervals work well alongside a quarterly review. This approach helps you spend your time where it's most valuable (which is not trying to figure out how marketing works).

Quarterly Review

Quarterly reviews allow you to analyze seasonal trends, assess long-term campaign impact, and refine your overall strategy. This in-depth analysis can reveal insights that weekly or monthly reports might miss, helping you set new goals for the coming quarters.

- Define the Wildly Important Goal (WIG) — what you're trying to do, and what winning looks like
- Create your marketing calendar to show the big picture
- Specify KPIs to ensure the strategy you're executing is aligned with your success

1 Hour Monthly Meeting

Monthly reports provide a broader view of campaign performance. Track lagging KPIs, like conversions and revenue, to assess overall success. Monthly reviews give small businesses time to analyze larger patterns without overwhelming the reporting process.

- Review key metrics — leading and lagging key performance indicators
- Discuss upcoming opportunities
- Pivot the marketing calendar to reflect reality (this is kind of important)

Weekly 15-Minute Check-In

Weekly check-ins should focus on leading KPIs, like website traffic and engagement rates. Monitoring these metrics frequently helps companies identify early trends and adjust tactics before issues arise. For example, a sudden drop in website traffic could signal a need for content updates or ad adjustments.

- Select bite-sized commitments — tasks for you to do to accomplish your WIG
- Celebrate your success — because you're killing it!
- Adjust to account for any misses

Final Thoughts

As we close the pages on this playbook, remember that digital marketing isn't about one-off tactics or temporary campaigns - it's a journey of building credibility, value, and relationships. This book has explored strategies designed to fit the realities of small businesses, where budgets, time, and resources are precious. In today's digital landscape, small business owners like you have the unique opportunity to connect authentically with customers, building a strong foundation that sustains growth and trust.

Revisiting Key Concepts

Each chapter has equipped you with actionable strategies for every part of your digital marketing process. From defining your buyer personas to crafting engaging content, you now have a toolkit for addressing real-world marketing challenges with precision. Whether it's mastering the marketing funnel, leveraging paid ads, or understanding SEO's nuances, the path to effective digital marketing demands commitment, consistency, and clarity.

Digital marketing requires that you be both a reliable marketer and a storyteller. Building and nurturing your own customer list, sharing your unique story, and consistently engaging across platforms are critical for small business marketing success. Each element is part of a system that, when executed with intention, can elevate your brand and drive real results.

Embracing the Marketing Mindset

Success in digital marketing comes down to the mindset you bring to each effort. Growth is the reward for consistency, experimentation, and resilience. You've seen that it's not about chasing trends or aiming for virality; it's about forging real connections and communicating your brand's unique value. With a long-term view, patience, and commitment, you'll see your marketing pay off in more leads, stronger brand recognition, and deeper customer loyalty.

Looking Forward

The digital landscape will continue to evolve, but the fundamentals will remain. As you apply these strategies, remember to stay adaptable and open to learning. Regularly evaluate what's working, refine your approach, and stay engaged with your audience's needs. The insights and practices here aren't static; they're dynamic, and your ongoing success will rely on your ability to adapt them over time.

Thank you for choosing this playbook as your guide. Your commitment to learning and implementing these strategies is an investment in your business's future. May your journey in digital marketing be rewarding and lead you toward sustainable growth and enduring success.

Glossary

Audience Segment: A group of people with similar traits, like age or interests, within a larger audience.

Backlink: The quantity and quality of links pointing to your site

Branded Pay-Per-Click: Ads that use a brand's name or product to appear higher in search results.

Business-to-Business (B2B): When businesses sell products or services to other businesses.

Business-to-Consumer (B2C): When businesses sell products or services directly to consumers.

Call to Action (CTA): Words or buttons that encourage people to take action, like "Buy Now" or "Sign Up."

Click-Through Rate (CTR): The percentage of people who click on an ad or link.

Conversion Rate Optimization (CRO): Making changes to a website to get more visitors to take action, like buying or signing up.

Cost Per Click (CPC): The cost a business pays each time someone clicks on its ad.

Cost Per Impression (CPM): The cost a business pays each time 1,000 people see its ad.

Customer Lifetime Value (CLV): The total money a customer is expected to spend with a business over their entire relationship.

Customer Relationship Management (CRM): A tool that helps businesses track and manage their relationships with customers.

Demographic: Information about people, like age, gender, or income.

Domain Authority (DA): A score showing how strong a website is in search engines, like Google.

Domain Name Registrar: A company that sells website names, like .com addresses.

Domain Name System (DNS): A system that connects website names to their correct IP addresses.

eCommerce: Buying and selling products or services online.

Engagement: The amount of time users spend on your content

Frequently Asked Questions (FAQ): A list of common questions and their answers.

Google Analytics: A tool that tracks and reports what visitors do on a website.

Google Search Console: A tool that helps track and improve a website's performance on Google.

Google Tag Manager: A tool that helps add and manage website tracking codes without changing the website's code directly.

Key Performance Indicator (KPI): A measure that shows how well a business is doing.

Lagging KPI: A measure that shows past results, like total sales.

Lead Value (LV): The average amount of money each lead could bring to a business.

Leading KPI: A measure that predicts future results, like new leads.

Long-Tail Keyword: A short phrase with three or more words that helps people find something specific online.

Marketing Campaign: A planned series of activities to promote a product or service.

Marketing Channel: A way to reach customers, like social media, email, or TV ads.

Marketing Qualified Lead (MQL): A person who shows interest in a product and might be ready to buy but needs more information.

Marketing Strategy: The plan for reaching customers and selling to them.

Multivariate Test: A type of A/B test that changes and compares different parts of something to see which combination works best.

Name, Address, Phone Number (NAP): Important contact information for a business.

Natural Language Processing (NLP): A technology that helps computers understand human language.

Nurturing Campaign: A series of messages to build a relationship with potential customers over time.

Organic Marketing: Free ways to promote a business, like social media posts or SEO.

Paid Marketing: Promoting a business by paying for ads or boosted content.

Pay-Per-Click (PPC): An ad where a business pays money each time someone clicks on it.

Pay-Per-Impression (PPM): An ad where a business pays money each time 1,000 people see it.

Podcast: An audio program available online that people can listen to.

Product Listing Ad (PLA): An ad that shows product info, like a picture, price, and description.

Profit: The money a business has left after paying all its costs.

Profit Margin (PM): The percentage of money a business keeps after paying its costs.

Referral Rate (RR): The percentage of customers who recommend the business to others.

Reputation: Links from trustworthy sources

Return on Investment (ROI): The money made back compared to the money spent.

Revenue: The total money a business makes from selling products or services.

RSS Feed: A tool that sends updates from websites, like news or blogs, to one place.

Sales Qualified Lead (SQL): A person who shows strong interest in buying and is ready for a sales team to contact.

Search Engine Optimization (SEO): The practice of improving a website so it shows up better in search results.

Search Engine Results Page (SERP): The page that shows the results after a search.

Sitemap: A list or map that shows all pages on a website.

Skyscraper Technique: Crafting content by researching existing high-performing posts, enhancing them, and then producing a superior version.

Software as a Service (SaaS): Software that people use over the Internet, often by paying a subscription.

Unqualified Lead: A person who may not yet be interested in buying or does not match the target customer profile.

Urchin Tracking Module (UTM): A small code added to a link to track where website visitors come from.

User Experience (UX): How easy and enjoyable it is to use a website or product.

User Interface (UI): The part of a product or website that people interact with, like buttons and menus.

Website Host: A service that stores and shows your website on the Internet.

Website Platform: Software used to build and manage a website, like WordPress.

Website Plugin: An extra feature that adds more tools to a website.

Website Template: A ready-made design layout for building a website quickly.

Website Theme: Software added to a Website Platform that controls how a website looks.

Wildly Important Goal (WIG): The most important goal a team or business focuses on to succeed.

Wireframe: A simple outline or sketch of a webpage to show where things will go.

Supplemental Content

Additional resources for this book can be downloaded at https://mazloy.com/win

TO: CHRIS

FROM: STEVE

NO AMOUNT OF KINDNESS,
NO MATTER HOW SMALL,
IS EVER FORGOTTEN.

About the Author

Christopher Mazurk

Christopher Mazurk is the Owner of Mazloy, LLC - a Marketing Consultancy in Orange County, CA. Chris has worked in Online Marketing since 1996. During this time, he has run successful campaigns for several Fortune 500 companies. These include Toyota, Sharp, Ingram Micro, and The Irvine Company. He has also worked with hundreds of small business owners. Everything from websites to videos, pay-per-click, organic listings, social media, and more. Chris is passionate about helping small businesses succeed through marketing. He also loves his wife, their dog, music, brewing beer, and playing hockey.

www.ingramcontent.com/pod-product-compliance
Lightning Source LLC
Chambersburg PA
CBHW070929210326
41520CB00021B/6853